"The prospect of reading Karl Barth's theo̶ and experienced theologians alike. The hi̶ time and our own, the complexity of his̶ debates about his work, and the sheer number of pages Barth produced can make it difficult to know where and how to begin. That's where this book comes in. David Guretzki has spent years helping students explore Barth's theology, and he has distilled the wisdom he has gained during these years into these pages. The result is an accessible and generous guide to Barth's theology that reduces the intimidation factor, answers common questions, and makes the task of reading Barth fun. I recommend this book for professors, students, pastors, and anyone else interested in reading Barth."
Keith L. Johnson, Wheaton College

"Beginning readers of Karl Barth will not find a better, more reliable, more accessible introduction to his theology than David Guretzki's *An Explorer's Guide to Karl Barth*. Guretzki knows Barth's theology so well that he can explain it without using a lot of technical jargon. The idea of including a list of Barth-related FAQ is a stroke of genius. I will certainly assign this book to my own students."
Joseph Mangina, professor of theology, Wycliffe College, Toronto

"Barth's *Church Dogmatics* is galactic in scope and grandeur: too vast to take in merely with the naked eye. As with the night sky, it requires the use of a telescope, where vast vistas are brought close. For a second one catches a glimpse of the whole in the part, only to leave the telescope behind, gaze up at the night sky, and again be reminded of the depth and grandeur of the whole—all the while holding on to the partial yet real insights provided by the telescope. Barth's theology is a universe and Guretzki has given us a glimpse through the telescope of his book of key constellations within Barth's cosmos, helping us gain an apprehension and understanding of the whole. This is a brilliant little book that will prove to be a useful tool for all those wanting to study Barth and his theology, especially those who are gazing upon his work for the first time."
Myk Habets, dean of faculty, head of Carey Graduate School, lecturer in systematic theology, Carey Baptist College

"This is a concise, lighthearted, judicious, and well-written introduction to Karl Barth's life and thought. Guretzki is a winsome and reliable guide for new explorers of Barth's work."

Adam Neder, Bruner-Welch Professor of Theology, Whitworth University

"One of the biggest challenges to studying the work of Karl Barth with genuine comprehension is simply getting started and moving in the right direction. In this volume, David Guretzki provides an ideal place for readers to begin, based on years of introducing his students to Barth's writings and theological ideas. A most welcome resource for those embarking on the journey of reading Barth as well as those seeking to teach them."

John R. Franke, theologian in residence, Second Presbyterian Church, Indianapolis, author of *Barth for Armchair Theologians*

"In this introductory guide to Karl Barth's life and thought, David Guretzki reliably acquaints readers in a welcoming fashion with many important themes in the theology of Karl Barth. Most notably, he helpfully points readers to Barth's own spiritually captivating analysis as one of the leading biblical and truly Christocentric theologians to appear since Augustine, Athanasius, or Thomas Aquinas. Anyone reading this book will see, with Guretzki, why so many serious Christian theologians today believe that 'one cannot claim to be engaged in the study of Christian theology without in some way engaging or becoming at least familiar with Karl Barth.'"

Paul D. Molnar, professor of systematic theology, St. John's University, Queens, New York

"For the interested but uninitiated reader, accessing Barth's theology is no easy task. Standard introductions and surveys of his theology remain accessible only to those generally familiar with it. The need for a more easily accessible entry into reading Barth has been longstanding. Guretzki's book satisfies this need. Not only is it concise, well written, and very balanced, it also points readers in the right directions in terms of further primary and secondary sources. This book is well worth acquiring!"

Archie Spencer, Trinity Western University, author of *The Analogy of Faith*

An Explorer's Guide to

KARL BARTH

DAVID GURETZKI

IVP Academic

An imprint of InterVarsity Press
Downers Grove, Illinois

InterVarsity Press
P.O. Box 1400, Downers Grove, IL 60515-1426
ivpress.com
email@ivpress.com

*InterVarsity Press® is the book-publishing division of InterVarsity Christian Fellowship/USA®, a
movement of students and faculty active on campus at hundreds of universities, colleges and schools
of nursing in the United States of America, and a member movement of the International Fellowship
of Evangelical Students. For information about local and regional activities, visit intervarsity.org.*

*Scripture quotations, unless otherwise noted, are from the New Revised Standard Version of
the Bible, copyright 1989 by the Division of Christian Education of the National Council of the
Churches of Christ in the USA. Used by permission. All rights reserved.*

*The image on p. 1 is "Karl Barth" by Ross Melanson. Used by permission. From the author's personal
collection.*
*Figure 3.1: Photo of Karl Barth's desk. Courtesy of Pittsburgh Theological Seminary. Photographer:
Michelle Y. Spomer. Permission granted for use.*
Figure 8.1: Kirchliche Dogmatik set. Jonund, 2014. Wikimedia Commons.

Cover design: Cindy Kiple
Interior design: Beth McGill
Images: Portrait of Karl Barth: Jessica Bergin
*   Karl Barth: National Portrait Gallery, Smithsonian Institution / Art Resource, NY
    handwriting: Barth's Romans commentary: Courtesy of the Center for Barth Studies,
    Princeton Theological Seminary on behalf of the Karl Barth Stiftung of Basel, Switzerland.
    gold compass: ©RUSSELLTATEdotCOM/iStockphoto
    compass: ©RUSSELLTATEdotCOM/iStockphoto*

ISBN 978-0-8308-5137-9 (print)
ISBN 978-0-8308-9433-8 (digital)

Printed in the United States of America ♾

 *As a member of the Green Press Initiative, InterVarsity Press is committed to
protecting the environment and to the responsible use of natural resources.
To learn more, visit greenpressinitiative.org.*

Library of Congress Cataloging-in-Publication Data
A catalog record for this book is available from the Library of Congress.

P   25   24   23   22   21   20   19   18   17   16   15   14   13   12   11   10   9   8   7   6   5   4   3   2   1

Y   34   33   32   31   30   29   28   27   26   25   24   23   22   21   20   19   18   17   16

To all past

and present members

of the Karl Barth Reading Group

at Briercrest College

and Seminary

There is no path from
which a man must not allow himself
to be summoned if a higher
necessity presents itself.

KARL BARTH,
CHURCH DOGMATICS III/2, XI.

Contents

Preface

There's no shortage of books on Karl Barth. If you've come here looking for the latest new insight or interpretation on the Swiss master, let me save you some time and disappointment by making it clear that this book was *not* written to make an original scholarly contribution to Barth studies. If that's what you're looking for, I would suggest you put the book down, back away, and keep looking . . .

However, if you're relatively unfamiliar with Karl Barth but want (voluntarily) to know more, or if you've been asked (involuntarily) to become familiar with him for a class or study group, then I hope this book will be of some assistance as you begin your study. Indeed, my primary objective in writing this book is to provide a guide—a handbook of sorts—explicitly designed to help new explorers of Karl Barth to get quickly acclimatized to his thought.

Because I've aimed this book at Barth beginners, I've focused less on the technical debates scholars are having (although I do mention a few of those along the way) and instead have given readers the most important information they need to keep moving forward. Consequently, I've also tried to keep the material as objective as possible (even if I know that it is finally impossible). Everyone has an opinion, and you, the reader, won't have a difficult time discerning that I am generally a fan of Barth's contributions, even if I don't follow him every step of the way. (Barth would be disappointed anyway to find out that anyone followed him at every single point. Dialogue, debate, and difference of opinion kept things interesting for Barth.)

Alongside the primary objective of creating an introductory-level book on Barth, I've tried to keep the prose light, tried to inject some occasional humor (though you will have to be the judge of whether there's anything humorous at all in this book—my teenagers groan at my "dad jokes," so I won't be *too* hurt if you groan, too), and tried to make the book as user friendly as possible.

Throughout this project, I've kept the image of an "explorer's guide" in mind. I find the metaphor helpful because of the way a good guide gives the traveler only enough information needed to enjoy the sights. Any guidebook that has vacationers spending more time reading it rather than enjoying the scenery is, in my mind, not a good guide. So, delicate balancing act that it has been, my goal is to produce something that readers can read as much or as little as they need in order to get them back to reading as much as they can from Barth himself. That means there is no need to read the book from start to finish, or even to read entire chapters. Read only what interests you or what is most pertinent in the moment. Then get back to reading Barth!

The book is divided into two parts. In part one, "Getting to Know Karl Barth," I provide enough insight into the man and his work for you to be better prepared to read him with profit (as in intellectually and theologically, not financially—theology doesn't have great prospects for that kind of profit). In this part, I outline a brief apologetic on why Barth is worth the effort, provide a brief biography of his life, give answers to some commonly asked questions about him, offer a glossary defining major ideas and persons that he interacted with, and then introduce readers to his life work through a tour of ten representative works carefully selected from the first couple of decades of his life.

In part two, "Exploring the *Church Dogmatics*," the focus turns to Barth's magnum opus. There I provide a primer on the nature and features of the work. I have also included an admittedly unusual chapter on how to use the *Church Dogmatics* for exegesis, for preaching, and for writing academic papers. This is followed by a chapter in which we take three paths through the *Church Dogmatics* for varying levels of interest, need, or time along with a brief commentary on the major themes and features of each part volume. In the last chapter, I provide a short annotated list of secondary sources and resources selected out of the mountain of secondary literature written on Barth. There are, after all, some texts that have more perennial or classic status that I believe readers should eventually read if they want to go further into the world of Barth studies.

I wish to thank several people who were instrumental in the production of this book. Thanks to David Congdon and the editorial staff at IVP for seeing the project as worthy in the first place and for encouraging me to get it done. Of course, I owe an ongoing debt of gratitude to my family for their love and support. My wife, Maureen, kept me writing at times when I didn't want to write, and my kids, Joey, Chiante, and Sierra, don't seem to be too damaged from the experience! Finally, I wish to thank all those people in the past decade who have been involved in the weekly Barth Reading Group at Briercrest College & Seminary in Caronport, Saskatchewan, Canada. I think there have been about sixty to eighty participants over the years—you know who you are. Thanks for allowing me to be your guide and colearner in our journeys through Barth's *Church Dogmatics.* It is to all of you, my fellow Karl Barth Reading Group pilgrims, that this book is dedicated.

Part One

Getting to Know
KARL BARTH

- 1 -

Why Karl Barth?

To celebrate our twenty-fifth anniversary, my wife and I decided to save up for a trip to Australia. In addition to seeing a travel agent, booking our tickets, and making sure we had vacation time booked, we also engaged in some planning on what we wanted to accomplish while we were traveling. We had only two weeks of vacation, and we wanted to make the best of it. So we bought a couple of those tourist guidebooks you see in the travel section at your local bookstore. It was exciting, and a bit overwhelming, to pore over all the opportunities! In the end, we embarked on our trip and enjoyed it immensely. But in the process we learned two vital lessons: first, two weeks is wholly insufficient to try to see Australia, and second, having those guidebooks saved us a lot of time in trying to figure out where we wanted to go and what we wanted to do on our journey.

It's my hope that this book will serve a little bit like one of those guidebooks—except that this one is designed to guide you on a journey through that continental land mass which I here awkwardly designate "Karl Barth's Theology." Newcomers to Karl Barth can find his cartload of books immensely intimidating, and so it is my goal to guide readers gently past some of the initial barriers that might discourage them from pressing on. In other words, I tried to write the book I wish I could have had in my first encounter with Barth. If only someone had tried to give me a basic understanding of what *dialectic* was, or what it meant when people called him a theologian of crisis. Whether this book will actually make it easier to go on an exploratory journey of Barth will be up to my readers to decide, but I offer it because of how enriching Karl Barth has been to my own theological development, thinking, and indeed, my Christian discipleship.

My Journey with Barth

Karl Barth was someone I encountered on a theological rabbit trail in my seminary education in the early 1990s. The topic I had chosen to research for a historical theology class was Augustine and the *filioque*. It was during my research that I found out that Karl Barth had written an extensive defense of the *filioque* in his monumental *Church Dogmatics*,[1] so I checked the first half-volume out of the library and began to read. Let's just say I was simultaneously overwhelmed by Barth's complex theological prose, yet unmistakably hooked by the beauty, depth, and breadth of his reflections. In fact, I became so enamored by Barth that eventually I pursued and finished a PhD degree in which I examined in depth the origin, meaning, and implications of Karl Barth's defense of the *filioque*.[2] Since then, I have continued to teach theology in a Canadian evangelical college and seminary and have found myself returning to Barth's work again and again. I have written several pieces in journals and reviews on Barth, and I even run a Karl Barth reading group that meets weekly to discuss a portion of his *CD*. As of this writing, we are celebrating our tenth anniversary as a group!

---

[1]Karl Barth, *Church Dogmatics*, 4 volumes in 13 parts, ed. Geoffrey Bromiley and T. F. Torrance (Edinburgh: T&T Clark, 1936–1962). Hereafter, all references to the *Church Dogmatics* will be in the following format: *CD* I/1, 100, i.e., *Church Dogmatics*, volume I, part 1, page 100. Generally, *CD* will also abbreviate *Church Dogmatics* in the text.

[2]If you're really interested, see David Guretzki, *Karl Barth on the Filioque* (Burlington, VT: Ashgate, 2009).

▶**Filioque:** The word *filioque* is Latin for "and the Son" and refers to a phrase included in certain sixth-century Latin versions of the Nicene Creed that was not in the original fourth-century Greek text. Consequently, Latins began to confess belief in the procession of the Holy Spirit from the Father *and the Son,* which eventually became a major factor in the split between Eastern and Western Churches. To see Barth's most complete comments on the filioque, see *CD* I/1, 473-87.

When I began writing this book, I decided to make one of two fundamental assumptions about you, the reader. Either you are interested in exploring Barth but don't really know where to start, or you are being forced to read Barth because your theology professor is making you! If you fit best in the former category, then I hope this guide will get you started posthaste. If you fit better in the latter category, I hope that what follows will help you understand why your professor wants you to get interested and learn something about Barth. Which begs the question: Why Barth?

A Case for Getting to Know Barth

Exploring Barth's theology is, without question, a daunting task. Most beginners are exposed to his *CD* and can be overwhelmed by its tiny print, its Latin and Greek citations, and its multiple volumes. Those factors alone can be enough to turn people away from Barth to someone a bit more accessible![3] But that makes me

---

[3]Fortunately, beginners are generally unaware of the even more intimidating fact that the Collected Edition (*Gesamtausgabe*) of Barth's works will consist of over six hundred longer and shorter writings. Although the collection is not yet complete, it already extends over fifty volumes. To see the volumes already included in the set titled *Karl Barth-Gesamtausgabe,* see www.tvz-verlag.ch/index.php?id=55&tx_commerce_pi1[catUid]=10.

sad. I really think Barth is worth the effort of getting to know, so
allow me the opportunity to provide a brief "apologetic" for why
those studying Christian theology need to spend some time getting
to know him.

There are many theologians who are worth getting to know, and
in any case, it has little to do with whether in the end you find
yourself agreeing with or aligned to the theologian or not. Far too
often, we are too quickly biased for or against theologians on the
basis of our theological teachers' advice. We all make recommenda-
tions and warnings based on those biases, including me, so you
might think that my case for Barth is just an inevitable part of my
own bias. But I hope you will see that my argument for reading
Barth is not just a matter of theological preference or style. There
are substantial reasons for why Barth *must* be engaged, even if in
the end we may come to radically different conclusions on various
issues or even on the value of Barth himself.

I can testify that there was (and still is, in some sectors) a real
bias in certain theological circles *against* Karl Barth. On the one
hand, the anti-Karl Barth bias I received in my earliest theological
education came from the theologically conservative end of the
spectrum, which essentially dumped Barth into the "liberal" camp,
despite his clear battle against his own liberal forebears. You see, I
was educated in the 1980s at a theologically conservative evangelical Bible college (the same school where I now teach) whose
teachers (with one really important exception) either knew nothing
about Karl Barth or, if they did, often warned us students to stay
studiously away from him, probably because their teachers had
told them to do the same. I discovered much later, when I was
going through some of my old college notes, that many of their
criticisms of Barth, while valid to a point, often echoed the critiques that theologians such as Cornelius Van Til had made against
Barth but that today have been either discredited or significantly

qualified.[4] Fortunately, this bias was eventually overcome in my case through one of my theology professors who actually assigned readings from Karl Barth in a couple of my seminary theology classes.[5] This is not to besmirch my earlier teachers (who I am sure were doing the very best for the Lord that they could do) but simply to indicate how very much things have changed in the past twenty or thirty years, even in the Canadian evangelical context in which I now find myself working.

On the other hand, there are those at the other end of the theological spectrum—those who see themselves more aligned with the liberal theological traditions— that have resisted Barth for very different reasons than my teachers did. For those schooled in the historical-critical methods of scriptural interpretation, it seemed as if Karl Barth was simply too theologically and exegetically naive. Although Barth was plainly aware of the findings of the critical biblical scholarship of his day, he often either rejected those conclusions out of hand or

EXPLORE FURTHER

For two relatively recent collections of evangelical engagements with Barth, see David Gibson and Daniel Strange, eds., *Engaging with Barth: Contemporary Evangelical Critiques*; and Bruce L. McCormack and Clifford B. Anderson, eds., *Karl Barth and American Evangelicalism.*

---

[4]See Cornelius Van Til, *Christianity and Barthianism* (Philadelphia: P&R, 1962). However, two recent essays have ably shown both the origins and shortcomings of Van Til's critique. See George Harinck, "'How Can an Elephant Understand a Whale and Vice Versa?' The Dutch Origins of Cornelius Van Til's Appraisal of Karl Barth," in *Karl Barth and American Evangelicalism*, ed. Bruce L. McCormack and Clifford B. Anderson (Grand Rapids: Eerdmans, 2011), 13-41; and D. G. Hart, "Beyond the Battle for the Bible: What Evangelicals Missed in Van Til's Critique of Barth," in *Karl Barth and American Evangelicalism*, ed. Bruce L. McCormack and Clifford B. Anderson (Grand Rapids: Eerdmans, 2011), 42-72.

[5]I wish to express public gratitude to Rev. Robert Seale, who was the first to introduce me to Karl Barth and who allowed me the latitude to make up my own mind about Barth's theological value.

wrote as if those findings simply didn't exist. In contrast to those working in my own tradition who thought Barth was simply too influenced by critical scholarship and was too quick to acknowledge the fallibility of the Bible and the Christian tradition, those working from within the liberal tradition thought Barth was too quick to jump to traditional, precritical, exegetical, and theological conclusions. For example, while many of Barth's contemporaries had jettisoned the idea of the virgin birth of Christ, Karl Barth continued to defend the virgin birth as "theologically fitting" even in a modern context.[6] The point here is that Karl Barth is one of those theologians who seems to have been consistently attacked from both his right and his left, either because he sounded too "liberal" or because he seemed too "theologically conservative and/or naive."

My argument here is not that everyone in the past was wrong about Barth and that we now understand Barth better from both sides of the theological spectrum and that we must now see Barth as the perfect middle position between liberal and conservative theologies. That would be silly. What I am arguing, however, is that regardless of the conclusions one ultimately makes about whether Barth is friend, foe, or somewhere in between, one cannot claim to be engaged in the study of Christian theology without in some way engaging or becoming at least familiar with Karl Barth. One need only do a survey of major theological works being produced in virtually every quarter of Christianity—Lutheran, Reformed, Baptist, Catholic, Anglican, Anabaptist, Eastern Orthodox, neo-liberal, neo-evangelical, radical orthodox, fundamentalist, liberationist, feminist, analytical, philosophical—and you are bound to run up against Karl Barth. In the end you don't have to like Barth, but you will be hard pressed to ignore him if you want to truly be theologically informed.

---

[6]See Dustin Resch, *Barth's Interpretation of the Virgin Birth: A Sign of Mystery* (Farnham, Surrey, England: Ashgate, 2012), 199-200.

Because Barth *is* widely engaged in the different sectors of Christian thought doesn't, however, automatically mean that he is *worth* being understood. We know that having a majority of people approve of something doesn't necessarily make it right or good. So, too, the fame or popularity (and I would admit that Barth is pretty popular these days) of a theologian is no guarantee either of her or his orthodoxy or relevance. So beyond his widespread appeal, why else should we study Barth? Though more could be adduced, I give you two of the most important theological reasons I can think of: because (1) Barth is thoroughly *Christ-centered*, and therefore, to be read with great spiritual benefit; and because (2) Barth is thoroughly *biblical*, and therefore to be taken seriously as a theologian of Scripture.

So what do I mean when I say that Barth is thoroughly *biblical*? To begin with, do not think I am claiming that everything Barth says aligns with Scripture. It would be naive at best and foolish at worst to attribute theological infallibility to a mere mortal. No, when I say Barth is thoroughly *biblical* I mean that Barth, perhaps with few peers in the history of the church, is both *committed to* and practically *uses* the Bible as the basis for his theology more than any theologian I know.[7] One only needs to peruse the index volume (as I will recommend at various points throughout this book) to become aware of how committed to and how much Scripture Barth practically engages in his *CD*. Not only does he explicitly mention or cite, according to my estimates, up to half of all of Scripture's verses, but there are implicit allusions to Scripture every step of the way. As Webster puts it, the *CD* "is best read as a set of conceptual variations upon scriptural texts and themes, sometimes explicitly tied to exegesis, sometimes more loose and indirect, but always

---

[7]I am by no means the first to suggest that Barth is essentially a *biblical* theologian. On this theme, see especially Thomas F. Torrance, *Karl Barth, Biblical and Evangelical Theologian* (Edinburgh: T&T Clark, 1990).

attempting to indicate what is already proclaimed in the prophetic and apostolic witness."[8]

Furthermore, when I assert that Barth is a *biblical* theologian, I mean that Barth explicitly *intends* to build his theological arguments and assertions up from the basis of his reading of the Bible and, more indirectly, yet intentionally, *avoids* as much as he is able to build his arguments on the basis of other sources. Whether or not in the end he succeeds in trying to excise, for example, philosophical assumptions from his work (or even whether such an objective is possible), at least Barth should be properly credited for his refreshingly self-critical efforts to do so. We may or may not agree with his assertions or his omissions, but we cannot ignore that at the very least he has intentionally and deliberately sought to make those statements on the basis of biblical evidence and not on the basis of cultural, philosophical, historical, or scientific evidence. Thus, if you value the role of Scripture and its authority in theology, and whether or not you agree that other sources can or should be ruled out in doing theology, Barth stands as one of the best exemplars of seeking to construct his theology under and submit his theology to the authority of Scripture. Therefore, I argue, he is someone to whom any Christian theologian should, at the very least, listen and respond. I suppose I see it this way: I may disagree vehemently with someone's interpretation of Scripture, but I will engage with anyone who explicitly seeks to make their case on the basis of Scripture and under the assumption of its authority. I see at least one of the most important of these *someones* in Karl Barth.

Barth as a *biblical* theologian can be understood at a more profound level. You see, for Barth the Bible was not simply a set of quotations about God and systematic theology was not simply

---

[8]John Webster, "Barth, Karl," in *Dictionary for Theological Interpretation of the Bible,* ed. Kevin J. Vanhoozer (Grand Rapids: Baker Academic, 2005), 83.

arranging those quotations in systematic and logical order. Rather, Barth was utterly convinced that God continued to speak to and transform us humans in our everyday world in and through the Bible. It was not simply a record of God's speaking in the past. As T. F. Torrance once eloquently put it, "For Barth true Biblicism meant accustoming himself to breathe the air of divine revelation . . . and to indwell its message in such a way that the truth of divine revelation became built into the very walls of his mind."[9] I believe Barth is worth learning from because I am convinced he so well illustrates not only what it means to discern what is written about God in the Bible but also how the Bible continues to be used by God to write and rewrite what we know about ourselves.

Learning a bit about Barth is also worth the effort because he is *Christ-centered.* Now, I realize it's fashionable to speak about being "Christ-centered" in many aspects of the Christian life. We speak of Christ-centered preaching or Christ-centered marriages or Christ-centered Christian education or even Christ-centered leadership. Yet such Christ-centeredness is not always easy to define, and the phrase is admittedly wearing thin in its descriptive power. I want to argue that Barth is an excellent example of what it means to be a truly *Christ-centered* theologian. What do I mean by this?

You've probably heard it mentioned in Christian circles that *Jesus* is the standard Sunday school answer children give when they don't know the answer to a question. Sometimes at my Barth reading group, I ask a question and answers aren't immediately forthcoming. After a moment or two of silence, sometimes someone will timidly whisper, "Jesus?" to which we all laugh, only to realize how often the answer is in fact true. The serious side of this little Christian inside joke is that *Jesus Christ* is, for Barth, not only the proper answer but also the proper question! Barth was not simply content

---

[9]Torrance, *Karl Barth,* 117-18.

to repeat the name of Jesus as a given but was convinced that Jesus Christ—the person, not just the words or the name—calls into question virtually everything that we think we know about God and his world.

We may believe, for example, that creation is everything that we know exists—the world, the stars, the trees, the animals, us, and so on. But Barth insists that such a perception is *not* true. Creation, Barth would argue, isn't just the stuff that God made: it's the whole context or environment in which God has chosen to enter into covenantal relationship with his creatures. And for Barth, that relationship is made possible and real at God's initiative in the one mediator, the man Jesus Christ. Thus, it's in meeting Jesus Christ that we come to know and understand the significance of this place we call our world—creation—a creation that was made *by* and *for* Jesus (cf. Col 1:16).

We may also believe that universally humans know what sin is. Everyone knows that we do some things right and other things wrong, and that the things that are wrong are sins. Right? Wrong—according to Barth. Barth insists that even the concept of sin cannot be properly understood apart from reference to God's living standard in the man Jesus. Barth even attempts to define sin as anything that is opposed to the obedience, exaltation, and glory of Christ.[10] That is, sin is not simply the failure to live up to the standard of a particular law or set of laws like the Ten Commandments (that is still, I daresay, the way most Christians think about sin—as a breach of a moral code), but a failure to live in obedience and in conformity to the image of God's Son, Jesus. Sin for Barth, therefore, is a failure to relate to God in the way that he has decided he wants to relate to us—in and through Jesus Christ.

---

[10]This view of sin is reflected in the very structure of the fourth volume of his *CD*. See the discussion of *CD* IV in chapter 8 below.

So you see, Jesus is not only the answer for Barth but also the question that calls into question all our presumed answers to what we think we already know about God and the world. Indeed, Barth so routinely and so regularly sought to work out his theology from the perspective of God's revelation of himself in the person of Jesus Christ that some of his critics labeled him a "christomonist" theologian,[11] one for whom Christology overshadowed or obliterated virtually every other theological theme. Barth personally disliked the term and preferred instead to speak of the "Christological concentration" in his thought, noting that "Christian doctrine, if it is to merit its name and if it is to build up the Christian church in the world as she must needs be built up, has to be exclusively and conclusively the doctrine of Jesus Christ."[12]

Barth is *Christ-centered* (or christocentric) because he stands as a model of what it means intentionally, often, and consistently to ask this question: What can we properly say about *this theological topic* as understood through the lens of God's self-giving and self-revelation of himself in Jesus Christ? As for me, one seeking to be a follower and disciple of Jesus Christ, Barth's christocentrism has been often a source

EXPLORE FURTHER
For a more thorough examination of Barth as christocentric, see Marc Cortez, "What Does It Mean to Call Karl Barth a 'Christocentric' Theologian?" On occasion, some have argued that Barth is ultimately a "pneumocentric" theologian, i.e., someone who puts the doctrine of the Holy Spirit at the center of his thought. See Philip J. Rosato, *The Spirit as Lord: The Pneumatology of Karl Barth.*

---

[11]For a brief discussion of the origin of the term *christomonism* and Barth's response to it, see Guretzki, *Barth on Filioque*, 42n131.

[12]Karl Barth, *How I Changed My Mind* (Richmond, VA: John Knox Press, 1966), 43.

of both theological and personal inspiration for me in my own biblical exegesis, teaching, writing, and sermon preparation.

I commend Barth to you not only because he is historically famous or even theologically ingenious but much more importantly because he is *spiritually valuable*: he is valuable because of how well he has tutored me in trying to see and measure everything through the lens of the living Lord Jesus Christ. I have often had the experience in reading Barth, either as in individual or in a group setting, when I have either had to pause and thank the Lord in prayer for who God is and what he has done by Christ and the Spirit, or be astonished at how rather *non*-Christ-centered I still am in my perceptions of life and this world. Barth, in other words, keeps pushing me to realize that the Christian life is being transformed increasingly and every day into someone who truly says, with John the Baptist, "He must increase, but I must decrease" (John 3:30 KJV). That is really what I think it means to be "Christ-centered," and it really is the best theological reason I can give you to spend more time reading Barth.

At this point, I still doubt that my case is watertight for why it's worth the effort and time of getting to know Karl Barth. But let me add one more piece of personal testimony: there has been no other theological writer who has done more to sharpen my own theological thinking and teaching than Karl Barth. Barth is not always the first one I consult on a question I am pondering—but he almost always is consulted. Barth is not always the one with whom I agree— but he almost always causes me to consider things I had not considered before. Barth doesn't always have something to say about a theological topic—but he usually does. Barth doesn't always have direct biblical support for his statements—but he almost always pushes me to consider whether in fact I have such support. And as much as Barth probably was not always the most authentic model follower of Jesus Christ, he most certainly has repeatedly forced me to consider whether I am truly a follower and witness of the Lord Jesus Christ. If for no other reason than this latter one, I will continue to read and teach Karl Barth. And I hope you will, too.

For Further Reading

Cortez, Marc. "What Does It Mean to Call Karl Barth a 'Christocentric' Theologian?," *Scottish Journal of Theology* 60 (2007): 127-43.

Gibson, Daniel, and Daniel Strange, eds. *Engaging with Barth: Contemporary Evangelical Critiques.* New York: T&T Clark, 2009.

Guretzki, David. *Karl Barth on the Filioque.* Burlington, VT: Ashgate, 2009.

McCormack, Bruce L., and Clifford B. Anderson, eds. *Karl Barth and American Evangelicalism.* Grand Rapids: Eerdmans, 2011.

Rosato, Philip J. *The Spirit as Lord: The Pneumatology of Karl Barth.* Edinburgh: T&T Clark, 1981.

Torrance, Thomas F. *Karl Barth, Biblical and Evangelical Theologian.* Edinburgh: T&T Clark, 1990.

- 2 -

Karl Barth

Who Was He?

There are widely varying opinions on the status of Karl Barth in theological history. Some readily announce that Barth is a twentieth century "church father" and one of the greatest, if not *the* greatest, theologians since the Reformation. Others are more reticent, thinking that ascribing greatness to Barth at this point in history is premature. They don't necessarily belittle his contribution, but argue that it's still too early to know his long-term impact in the unfolding of Christian history to come. Still others discern that Barth is one of the more dangerous, if not *the* most dangerous, threats to Christian orthodoxy in modern history.

But whatever one's theological assessment of his significance (an assessment we will resist making this early in the book), it is always good to situate a theologian's contribution in the broader context of history. When we do so, we remember that our battles are likely not theirs and that our ultimate assessment of them must not fail at least to consider their life history. So we "begin at the beginning," as Barth liked to say, and seek here to provide a brief account of his life.

Karl as a Child

Karl Barth's life began and ended in his hometown, Basel, Switzerland. He was a firstborn son and came into this world on May 10, 1886, to parents Johann Friedrich ("Fritz") and Anna Katharina (née Sartorius).[1] It was almost as if Karl were destined to be an academic, as his father was a professor of theology and his mother was the granddaughter of a professor of literature.

Karl was known as a boisterous young man who was both a dreamer and a fighter. His teachers testified that he often daydreamed in class and consequently often had to stay in for detention for failing to complete his schoolwork. He was also known to enjoy getting into fights with some of the local boys, so much so that Karl became the leader of a small gang of boys. Karl's band of fighters eventually got into a feud with another gang led by a boy named Martin Werner, who, ironically, also eventually became a theologian!

In between dreaming and fighting, Karl also took up poetry and playwriting. Barth's most important biographer, Eberhard Busch, called the young Karl a "fighter and a poet."

Karl the Pupil

Barth began his theological education in 1904 at the university in Berne, Switzerland. The decision to attend Berne was at Fritz Barth's insistence. Though young Karl resisted, he eventually acquiesced. Once Barth felt his obligations to honor his father's wishes were fulfilled, he moved to Berlin where he started to soak up the lectures of the great dogmatic historian and theologian Adolf von Harnack (1851–1930), a professor to whom Barth was drawn more than any other of his teachers.

---

[1] Eberhard Busch, *Karl Barth: His Life from Letters and Autobiographical Texts* (Grand Rapids: Eerdmans, 1976), 497-98. All details for this short biography are derived from Busch's text, the most complete biography of Barth we have.

In Barth's day it was common for students to study at various universities, so, again at the insistence of his father who was concerned with the liberal influence at Berlin, Karl moved for a brief stint to Tübingen in 1907. Unfortunately for father Fritz, young Karl remained even more unconvinced by the more theologically conservative faculty he encountered at Tübingen and so quickly moved on to Marburg where in late 1907 he became a pupil of Wilhelm Herrmann, one of the most revered professors of dogmatics of the day. Under Herrmann, Barth learned of the intersection of theology and politics—an interest that never left him his entire life. It was during this time that Barth also became acquainted with Rudolf Bultmann and Ernst Troeltsch, both of whom Barth would later enter into longstanding theological disputation. While at Marburg, Barth published his first theological article in 1909 in the *Journal for Theology and Church* (*Zeitschrift für Theologie und Kirche*), titled "Modern Theology and Working for the Kingdom of God." Barth would later point to this article as evidence of what was then his utter and complete support of the program of modern theology, particularly as he had learned it from Herrmann and Harnack.

Barth the Political Pastor

After completing his theological education, some of Barth's peers were surprised to hear him announce his intention to move into pastoral work. And so, in the autumn of 1909, Barth became an assistant pastor in the Reformed church in Geneva at the same church where the great Reformer, John Calvin, had preached. Barth stayed at Geneva for two years, during which he learned the pastoral ropes, especially the art of preparing sermons, which he thoroughly enjoyed. He himself recollected especially his series on the epistle of James. As sermons, they tended to be quite academic in nature, and Barth later confessed that he doubted the great Calvin himself would have likely approved either of their form or content.

While in Geneva, Karl met young Nelly Hoffmann, a student and accomplished violinist in the confirmation class he was teaching. Karl and Nelly were engaged in 1911 when Nelly was only 18 years old. They eventually married in July 1913. Together, Karl and Nelly had one daughter (Franziska) and four sons (Markus, Christoph, Matthias, and Hans).

In 1911, between his engagement and wedding, Barth moved to Safenwil, Switzerland, where he became the sole pastor of a small village church. At the time, Safenwil was a small industrial town facing serious economic hardship. Barth became politically involved in the labor union movement, and even became a member of the Social Democrat party, which sought to bring social and economic relief to the everyday workers, thus earning Barth the epitaph of being a "red pastor." Even though Barth eventually left church ministry to became an academic dogmatic theologian, his concern for matters political and their intersection with the reign (kingdom) of God never left him.

Barth spent just over a decade at Safenwil, during which he underwent what most Barth scholars now see as a significant conversion away from the theological liberalism he had adopted from his divinity professors. However, Barth, together with his close pastor friend Eduard Thurneysen (pronounced, "Tur-NYE-zen"), knew that leaving liberalism did not necessarily mean adopting the "positive theology" that his father had hoped he would adopt. But what was the alternative?

It was during an extended study of Plato, Paul, and Kierkegaard during the years of the Great War (World War I) that the pastoral pair, Barth and Thurneysen, discovered a "strange world within the Bible." More specifically, Barth spent a number of intense months studying the epistle to the Romans accompanied by his own notes—a furiously written biblical commentary that turned out quite unlike most commentaries of the day. That commentary—

Barth's first edition of *The Epistle to the Romans* (German, *Der Römerbrief*) published in 1919—became one of the most significant public evidences that Barth had abandoned the liberal leanings of his teachers. The release of the commentary eventually launched him into the theological limelight. After gaining increased attention during a series of lectures delivered in both Switzerland and Germany, Barth was offered a teaching post at a theological faculty in Germany. Barth accepted the offer and left the pulpit in Safenwil for the podium in Göttingen in 1921. It was during this tumultuous period that the alternative to liberalism began to emerge: the theology of crisis, or dialectical theology (see **dialectic** in chapter four).

Barth the Professor

Prior to leaving Safenwil for Göttingen, Barth completed an extensive revision of his Romans commentary, which was eventually published in the second year of his first professorship in 1922. Barth's position at Göttingen was chair of Reformed theology in what was predominantly a Lutheran school. At first, Barth spent his podium time lecturing on biblical exegesis of New Testament books, while in his study he immersed himself in the dogmatic tradition of Reformed theology—an area of study he realized had been lacking in his own theological education.

By 1924, Barth finally began teaching seminars on dogmatics, the lectures of which would much later be published as the *Göttingen Dogmatics*. While Barth continued to lecture and write, he met Charlotte ("Lollo") von Kirschbaum, a Red Cross sister from Munich who had great interest in theology. Charlotte eventually, though not without some controversy and family tension, became Barth's lifelong research assistant, who also took up residence in the Barth household for many years.

When Barth's fame grew as a cutting-edge theologian who was bucking the theological establishment of the German universities, he again received an invitation to take up a post in Münster, Germany. While in Göttingen, Barth had contended with his Lutheran colleagues, but now in Münster, he was introduced to the intellectual and dogmatic challenges of the Roman Catholic professors teaching there. During this time, he increasingly understood that his task as a Reformed theologian was to engage, and indeed, counter, the Roman Catholic wing of Christian theology. The new context and the pushback he received from his Catholic colleagues convinced Barth that he needed to start his dogmatic project all over again—a task that he took up with vigor mixed with frustration. Most importantly for the so-called *Christian Dogmatics in Outline* (*Die christliche Dogmatik im Entwurf*), which he began at Münster, Barth felt that he needed to bring his understanding of Jesus Christ even more into the center of his thinking. And so it was at Münster that the primary structure was formed of what would eventually become his magnum opus, the *Church Dogmatics* (*Kirchliche Dogmatik*). But this was not to happen without at least one or two major detours and distractions.

In 1930, Barth yet again took up an invitation to join the prestigious faculty at the University of Bonn as the chair of systematic theology, a post he held until 1935. It was, of course, during this decade that Germany was going through the tumultuous rise of National Socialism led by Adolf Hitler preceding the outbreak of World War II.

The move to Bonn resulted in Barth starting, for a third time, on a "new and improved" version of his dogmatics—the *CD* on which Barth would work for the remainder of his life. His tenure at Bonn was also one of the most politically and theologically pivotal moments in Barth's career. In 1934, a contingent of representatives from the Lutheran and Reformed wings of the church in Germany joined forces to create the Confessing German Evangelical Church, which was in essence an attempt to resist what they deemed to be the highly destructive and dangerous theological and political direction of the "reforms" of the German National Church under Hitler's regime.

Figure 2.1. Karl Barth stamp, commemorating the 100th anniversary of his birth (author's collection)

In May 1934, the Confessing Church joined together to respond to the threats of the German National Church and produced the Barmen Declaration—a jointly adopted confession of faith resisting the illegitimate encroachment of the state into theological and ecclesiastical life.[2] Although the official Barmen Declaration was released without authors' names attached, it is widely acknowledged that Barth was its principal architect and author. Shortly thereafter, when Barth refused to provide an

---

[2]The text of the Barmen declaration can be found online at www.sacred-texts.com/chr /barmen.htm.

unqualified oath of allegiance to the *Führer* (i.e., Hitler) in 1935, he was removed from his teaching post and unceremoniously escorted out of Germany.[3] Barth returned to his homeland, Switzerland, where he lived out the remainder of his days teaching at his hometown university in Basel.

In the years following Barth's return to Basel, he worked diligently and consistently on his *CD,* the massive multivolume work that he never finally finished, which will be the focus of the second half of this guide. It was during his last thirty-plus years that Barth received numerous honorary doctorates, international awards, and worldwide media recognition, including being featured on the cover of *Time* magazine on the April 20, 1962, edition.[4] Barth rarely strayed from his hometown, though he did make his one and only trip to the United States in early 1962. He was also privileged to have an audience with Pope Paul VI in 1966. Karl Barth died sometime on the evening of December 9 or morning of December 10, 1968. Even on his last day, he continued to work on a lecture he had been asked to deliver—a lecture that remained unfinished and undelivered but which once again sought to testify to the center of his theological and life focus: the Lord Jesus Christ.

For Further Reading

If you wish to get more into the details of Barth's life, I recommend one of the following.

Short

Jüngel, Eberhard. *Karl Barth, a Theological Legacy.* Philadelphia, PA: Westminster Press, 1986, 22-27.

Webster, John. *Barth.* London and New York: Continuum, 2000, 1-19.

---

[3]See also "Was Barth the sole author of the Barmen Declaration?" in chapter 3.
[4]See the cover at http://content.time.com/time/covers/0,16641,19620420,00.html.

Medium
Franke, John R. *Barth For Armchair Theologians*. Louisville, KY: Westminster John Knox Press, 2006.

Long
Busch, Eberhard. *Karl Barth: His Life from Letters and Autobiographical Texts*. Grand Rapids: Eerdmans, 1976.

- 3 -

Frequently Asked Questions About Karl Barth

Entering the world of Karl Barth can be intimidating, and while my experience has been that (most) Barth aficionados are pretty patient with novices, it does help to get answers to some of the basic questions that come up over and over again. Thus, the "frequently asked questions" (FAQ) I cover in this chapter are real-world questions that I have been asked in the past, along with a few more that I wish would get asked more often. It was difficult to know how to arrange the questions, and though there are some that seem to logically follow another, for the most part there was no real logical order other than the order in which I thought of them! Enjoy!

FUN FACT

Barth sounds like "Bart" (as in Simpson), not like "Darth" (as in Vader). Avoid embarrassment and just imagine Karl Barth going to work on Bart Simpson's skateboard and you'll never go wrong.

Was Barth a liberal theologian?

In his earliest years, yes. Later, not so much. Barth took his earliest theological training under some of the best scholars that German liberal theology had to offer. In essence, liberal theology sought to interpret the biblical text in light of the best advances of critical scholarship available. It sought to make sense of the historical and cultural contexts in which the Bible was written, the way in which sources underlying the texts informed the text, and the way in which the biblical texts found their way into their final form. Liberal theology also sought to better understand the history of Christian doctrine over the ages and how historical context through the centuries influenced how and what theologians and the church taught about what they thought the Bible said about God and the world. In essence, liberal theology took the *historical* nature of the Bible and Christianity very seriously and understood that both the Bible and Christian theology were subject to ongoing development and change.

Barth's most well-known teacher in the liberal tradition was probably the historian of dogma Adolf von Harnack. Some of Barth's early writings reveal his affinity for the methods and findings of modern liberal scholarship. However, at the outbreak of the Great War (World War I) in 1914, Barth was uncomfortable with what appeared to be his own theological teachers' nationalistic justification of the war effort. It is now widely recognized that Barth broke with his liberal teachers somewhere around 1915 while he was serving as pastor in Safenwil, Switzerland. It was then that his distinctive "dialectical" form of theology began to emerge, which was most clearly evident in his early commentaries on Romans.[1]

---

[1]For more on Barth's break with liberalism, see Bruce L. McCormack, *Karl Barth's Critically Realistic Dialectical Theology: Its Genesis and Development, 1909-1936* (Oxford: Clarendon Press, 1995), 117-25; and Gary Dorrien, *The Barthian Revolt in Modern Theology: Theology Without Weapons* (Louisville, KY: Westminster John Knox Press, 2000), 42-46.

Unlike his liberal forebears that saw the Bible as fundamentally an ancient text stranded in the past, Barth read Romans as an instrument by which God's very own word could be heard today, directly confronting the church in its beliefs and actions.

Was Barth a neo-orthodox theologian?

The best answer is, no, Barth was not neo-orthodox. But Barth has been and still is often called neo-orthodox, so some explanation is required.

The term *neo-orthodoxy* did not arise in continental Europe, or as a term by which Barth self-identified, but was used mainly in the English-speaking world of Great Britain and North America to designate Barth and others' distinctive theological style. There is evidence the term was originally a derogatory one meant to signal that those in the so-called neo-orthodox camp used traditional, orthodox language but imported alien meaning to that language. The term neo-orthodox eventually was used to lump together a broad range of thinkers, including Rudolf Bultmann, Friedrich Gogarten, Paul Tillich, Emil Brunner, and Reinhold Niebuhr, even though most of these had sharp disagreements on many issues. Generally speaking, designating these thinkers together as "neo-orthodox" has been increasingly viewed as unhelpful or even misleading. Barth himself repudiated the term as applied to himself.[2]

So Barth isn't liberal and isn't neo-orthodox. What, then, is he?

It's my hope that as you learn to read Barth (as with any seminal thinker), you will discover that what makes him unique is that he does not fit easily under predetermined labels. But if I had to pigeonhole him, I would say that Barth is modern in method,

---

[2]*CD* III/3, 11.

orthodox in confession, trinitarian in theological structure, biblical in orientation, christological in focus, dialectical in style, Reformed in soteriology, catholic (but not Catholic) in ecclesiology, scholastic in precision, systematic in approach, pastoral in intention, ecumenical in recognition, joyful in disposition, and Christian in commitment. Does that help?

> While on his one and only trip to the United States, Barth was given an opportunity to fire a Civil War–era musket, which he did. He then joked he had fired the last shot in the American conflict! Barth was also an avid reader of Civil War history. Source: Karl Barth, *How I Changed My Mind* (Richmond, VA: John Knox Press, 1966), 84–85.

I've heard that Barth's longtime assistant, Charlotte von Kirschbaum, wrote large parts of the *Church Dogmatics*. Is that true?

It is undeniable that Charlotte von Kirschbaum, who lived in the household with Karl and his wife Nelly from 1929 until 1966, played a significant role in the production of the *CD*. Von Kirschbaum met Barth during his professorship at Göttingen in 1924. At the time, she was a twenty-five-year-old Red Cross nurse who had shown a growing interest in theology. As they became more acquainted, Barth encouraged Charlotte ("Lollo" as he later called her) to take secretarial training—which she did. Eventually she became Barth's longtime assistant who was charged with gathering research and creating drafts of many of the small-print sections that Barth later edited and rewrote as he saw necessary. She also prepared materials for Barth's lectures and took some responsibility in helping him keep up with his correspondence. In this regard, von Kirschbaum rightly deserves credit for the role she played in the writing of the *Church Dogmatics*. Indeed, Barth draws attention to von Kirschbaum's contribution in the preface to *CD* III/3 where he notes, "She has devoted no less of her life and powers to the growth of this work than I have myself." Nevertheless, it will not be the last time that research assistants (and administrative assistants of all types) do not get their name on the spine of the book or as a coauthor in the journal article—rightly or wrongly.

While we are on the matter of Charlotte von Kirschbaum, I've also heard that she and Karl Barth had at best, an inappropriate, and at worst, an adulterous, relationship. How can we then trust his theology?

Those who have examined the history of Karl and Charlotte's relationship have come to differing interpretations about what really took place between them. I can't claim to have enough insight to take either side here, but it is almost certain that there was some level of intimate inappropriateness, even if they (and we don't know for sure) never were involved sexually. What we do know for certain is the following: (1) Karl and his wife Nelly stayed together for life; (2) there was undoubtedly a degree of marital tension in

EXPLORE FURTHER
For two books that view the Barth/von Kirschbaum relationship from quite different perspectives, see Suzanne Selinger, *Charlotte von Kirschbaum and Karl Barth: A Study in Biography and the History of Theology*; and Renate Koebler, *In the Shadow of Karl Barth: Charlotte von Kirschbaum*.

the household with Charlotte present; (3) Karl and Nelly reconciled in their latter years; (4) Karl and Nelly together visited Charlotte in a nursing home in her final years; (5) Karl, Nelly, and Charlotte are all buried together, with Nelly's approval, in the same family plot; and (6) household and living arrangements in Swiss Germany in the early to mid-twentieth century were very likely different than ours, so reading back our expectations of what was and was not appropriate is very likely problematic.

What does this mean for our reception of Barth's theology? I do not have an easy answer for anyone, and I suppose each reader needs to make a decision about whether Barth's moral failings disqualify him as a theologian from whom we can learn. That said, I also take comfort in knowing that God used deceivers (Jacob), cowards (Moses), adulterers (King David), traitors (apostle Peter), and murderers (apostle Paul) to carry out his redemptive plans, and even sometimes to serve as authors of Scripture. I, for one, *am* troubled by the fact that Barth seemed to be involved in morally questionable behavior, but I suppose I am troubled even more greatly by my own. God have mercy on me, a sinner. I just pray that the hundreds of students I have taught, and the hundreds of readers of my books and articles, will learn something, by God's Holy Spirit, of Jesus Christ and his demands of discipleship on their lives, despite my own moral failures and my own flawed discipleship. Whatever the case, I believe that Barth was a follower of Jesus and was, like us all, imperfect in his discipleship. That is no excuse, but simply a statement of what I think is reality.

Did Barth ever change his mind?

If you count his break from liberalism in the 1920s, most definitely. After that initial major change of mind, he changed his mind again at times, though he was reticent to admit it. Barth tended to insist that after he had broken with his liberal teachers, his thought forms remained essentially the same for the rest of his life, even while highlighting some things with greater clarity and letting other things fade more into the background.[3]

EXPLORE FURTHER
For some of the early signs of Barth's change of mind on baptism, most fully revealed in *CD* IV/4, see Karl Barth, *The Teaching of the Church Regarding Baptism*.

Barth's most (in)famous change of mind beyond his move away from liberalism was his stance on baptism as represented in volume IV/4 of the *CD*. Barth explicitly states in the preface that he had moved away from the sacramental understanding of baptism (including his support for infant baptism), a stance he had clearly held earlier in his life.

But if you want to know more about whether and how Barth changed his mind, see a collection of autobiographical essays gathered together under the title, you guessed it, *How I Changed My Mind*.[4]

FUN FACT

Barth was once asked by a BBC interviewer what he would have been if he hadn't become a theologian. Barth's response: A traffic policeman. Source: Donald K. McKim, *How Karl Barth Changed My Mind* (Eugene, OR: Wipf & Stock, 1998), 44.

---

[3]See Karl Barth, "The Humanity of God," in *The Humanity of God* (Richmond, VA: John Knox Press, 1960), 37-65.

[4]Karl Barth, *How I Changed My Mind* (Richmond, VA: John Knox Press, 1966).

Why did Barth write so much? Couldn't he have said it shorter?

Believe it or not, this is truly one of the most frequently asked questions I have gotten from students who are first introduced to Barth. Mangina answers this question much better than I can manage here,[5] but at the very least remember that Barth worked and wrote in a different time and age where scholars were actually expected to write prolifically and were unencumbered by the often crushing administrative duties today's educators are expected to perform. More substantially, Barth wrote so much because he understood that the object of his inquiry (God, who is really a living Object, and thus a living Subject who addresses us) is by definition infinitely greater than any human words can describe. At one point, Barth put it this way: "In respect of the *circulus veritatis Dei* ["circle of the truth of God"] we have no last word to speak. We can only repeat ourselves. We can, therefore, only describe Him again, and often, and in the last resort infinitely often."[6]

An image here might be helpful. Imagine being given the job, without camera or smartphone in hand, of trying to report back to friends who have never been to the Sistine Chapel what it was like to experience and observe Michelangelo's paintings on the ceilings. You would likely be hard pressed to keep it short, especially if you wanted make note of the beauty and genius of how the artist portrayed various characters, scenarios, colors, movements, nuances, and backgrounds, not to mention trying to take into account how a portion of the painting looked at different times of day under different lighting. For Barth, the attempt to comment on and describe the exquisite beauty and majesty of God meant simply that he needed to write what he could from every angle possible. Consequently, because his Subject was so gloriously beautiful and infinite,

---

[5] Joseph L. Mangina, *Karl Barth: Theologian of Christian Witness* (Louisville, KY: Westminster John Knox, 2004), 23-24.
[6] *CD* II/1, 250.

there is no reason to think that Barth could have ever seen his job as complete. And so he wrote—and wrote—and wrote—about the God he saw witnessed to in Scripture, and he hoped we would catch a glimpse of that same God ourselves.

Interestingly, Barth actually sought to defend his voluminous writing, so here is his answer:

> A good deal has already been said about the size both of the [*Church Dogmatics*] as a whole and also of each of its constituent parts. It may be conceded that the Bible itself can put things more concisely. But if dogmatics is to serve its purpose, then I cannot see how either I myself, or any of my contemporaries known to me, can properly estimate the more concise statements of the Bible except in penetrating expositions which will necessarily demand both time and space. . . . Yes, for a right understanding and exposition there is need of a thorough elucidation. May it not be that I have been too short and not too long at some important points?[7]

FUN FACT

Barth was a fan of the British mystery author and lay theologian Dorothy L. Sayers. He even translated some of Sayers's essays into German. Source: Laura K. Simmons, *Creed Without Chaos: Exploring Theology in the Writings of Dorothy L. Sayers* (Grand Rapids: Baker Academic, 2005), 12.

[7]*CD* II/2, ix.

Was Barth the sole author of the Barmen Declaration?

For the most part, yes, but not quite. The famous Barmen Declaration was written in 1934 as an official joint document of Lutheran
and Reformed churches. It was designed to prepare the confessing
Christians in Germany to stand firm against Hitler's anti-Semitic,
white supremacist ideology. Although Barth is (rightly) credited as
being the main author of Barmen, it is more accurate to say that the
original theses were outlined by Barth on May 16, 1934, while Barth
was meeting with Lutheran theologians Thomas Breit and Hans
Asmussen. As the day went, Barth reports that his friends had a nap
while he, "fortified by strong coffee and one or two Brazilian cigars,"
wrote the draft of the declaration. However, when the Synod of the
Confessing Church met May 29–31, 1934, the final version of the
declaration was hammered out almost without reference to Barth's
presence. So yes, most properly, Barth was responsible for the "first
draft" of the Barmen Declaration, even though the final text was
the result of the work of a committee.[8]

Was Barth really kicked out of Germany for refusing to declare an unconditional oath of allegiance to Hitler?

As often happens in the retelling of historically significant events,
versions of the story become more dramatically retold than how it
actually happened. In Barth's case, in late 1934 while teaching at
Bonn, Germany, all government employees, which included university professors, were required to give an oath of loyalty to the
Führer (Hitler). Barth did not refuse to give an oath of loyalty but
did ask that his oath be qualified in such a way that he would swear
allegiance to the *Führer* "only within my responsibilities as an Evangelical Christian." In other words, Barth reserved the right to refuse

---

[8]For an account of Barth's involvement with the Barmen Declaration, see Eberhard
Busch, *Karl Barth: His Life from Letters and Autobiographical Texts* (Grand Rapids:
Eerdmans, 1976), 245-46.

to do something that he felt transgressed his understanding of his loyalty to Christ and to Scripture as he understood them. His proposal was presented to the appropriate officials but was turned down, after which his position as professor was suspended. He was tried before three judges, found guilty, sentenced, and eventually dismissed from his post, after which he was required to leave the country. Barth returned to Basel under a police escort, with whom he had a friendly chat about the gospel, in March 1935.[9]

Was Karl Barth a universalist?

You'd think a simple yes or no would suffice. But you'd be wrong.

More specifically, does Barth believe that in the end (eschatologically speaking) everyone (and everything) will be eternally restored to a right relationship to God? Or if you are from the evangelical tradition (as I am), does Barth believe everyone will be saved?

A small cottage industry of Barth interpreters has sought to answer this question and all its variations definitively—with no clear consensus yet reached. Yours truly has even tried to contribute a piece to this puzzling question.[10]

My position on this question is, really, to take Barth at his own word:

We should be denying or disarming that evil attempt and our own participation in it if, in relation to ourselves or others or all men, we were to permit ourselves to postulate a withdrawal

---

[9]The story of Barth's exodus from Germany was recounted in a talk given by Eberhard Busch during the annual Karl Barth Conference, Princeton Theological Seminary, Princeton, NJ, June 22, 2010. For more detail on Barth's dismissal from Bonn, see Busch, *Karl Barth*, 253-60.

[10]David Guretzki, "Kerygmatic Hope: Another Look at Barth's Resistance to Universalism," in *Revisioning, Renewing, Rediscovering the Triune Center: Essays in Honor of Stanley J. Grenz*, ed. Derek J. Tidball, Brian S. Harris, and Jason S. Sexton (Eugene, OR: Wipf & Stock, 2014), 175-94. See also David Guretzki, "'Depart from Me!' Eternal Judgment in Christological Perspective," *Canadian Evangelical Review* (2009): 17-37.

of the threat [of the condemnation of humans] and in this
sense to expect or maintain an *apokatastatsis* or universal
reconciliation as the goal and end of all things. *No such postulate can be made even though we appeal to the cross and
resurrection of Jesus Christ.* Even though theological consistency might seem to lead our thoughts and utterances most
clearly in this direction, we must not arrogate to ourselves
that which can be given and received only as a free gift.[11]

In other words, though we might wish for universalism to be true,
and even if it seems the most theologically consistent thing to do
in light of Christ's status as Savior of the world, we can't make a
declaration that God will in fact save everyone.

In light of the above, I believe that it is improper to designate
Barth a universalist against his own denial of it. Yes, some insist that
Barth's theology logically leads to such a conclusion[12]—they might
even be right that logical consistency demands that conclusion. But
theological consistency was important for Barth only secondarily
to theological faithfulness to what he understood to be revealed. So,
from the perspective of what it appears that Barth *affirmed* (and
not just what we think he *should* have confirmed or denied), Barth
cannot properly be called a universalist. That doesn't end the
conversation, but I think it is the most honest starting point.

Beyond this, the question, "Is Barth a universalist?" has a few
more things that need to be considered: (1) The answer to this
question depends greatly on what is meant by "universalism" or the
concept of "being saved." Barth doesn't always align with the

---

[11]*CD* IV/3.1, 477, emphasis added.

[12]See, for example, Oliver Crisp, "On Karl Barth's Denial of Universalism," in *Retrieving
Doctrine: Essays in Reformed Theology* (Downers Grove, IL: IVP Academic, 2010),
116-30. For a response to Crisp, see W. Travis McMaken, "Review of Oliver D. Crisp,
Retrieving Doctrine: Essays in Reformed Theology (IVP Academic, 2010)," *Koinonia:
The Princeton Theological Seminary Graduate Forum* 23 (2011): 123-26.

assumptions often underlying the question; (2) there is an undeniable "universalist bent" in Barth inasmuch as he prefers to speak of the victory of Jesus Christ and that all are elected in Christ, even as Christ is both the elect and reject for us; (3) it isn't at all clear that when Barth says all are elect in Christ that this is to be equated with the idea that all are saved.

I believe that a proper interpretation of Barth leads us to conclude that at most, Barth went to the grave hoping that one day God would save all. But I also know that Barth refused to make statements about the eschatological destiny of all of humanity on the principle that he believed that only Jesus Christ, the Judge who is to come, could and will ultimately make those judgments. As I have put it elsewhere, Barth would have us preach that Jesus Christ is Victor and Savior of all, but leave the final judging of individual destinies up to Jesus Christ on the day when he returns.[13]

Did Barth really say that the Bible only "becomes" the Word of God but is not the Word of God in itself?

This is one of those common sayings that has long been attributed to Barth, usually by some of his evangelical and fundamentalist critics in North American contexts. The reason it continues to be repeated is because, well, Barth did say that the Bible becomes the Word of God. For example, he says, "The Bible is God's Word to the extent that God causes it to be His Word, to the extent that he speaks through it."[14] Or, more explicitly,

Without wanting to deny or even limit their character as God's Word we must bear in mind that the Word of God is mediated here, first through the human persons of the prophets and apostles who receive it and pass it on, and then

---

[13]See Guretzki, "Kerygmatic Hope," 193.
[14]*CD* I/1, 109.

through the human persons of its expositors and preachers, so that *Holy Scripture and proclamation must always become God's Word in order to be it.*[15]

In the context of these passages and others, Barth emphasizes that the Bible can only be said to be God's Word inasmuch as God actually uses it to reveal to humans God's own self. As he puts it, "In this event the Bible is God's Word."

However, this is one of those things repeated about Barth that can so easily be taken on its own or seriously misunderstood without going on to read further and in larger context. As early as his *Göttingen Dogmatics,* Barth had already insisted: "Let us begin at once with the unavoidable insight that the Bible cannot come to be God's Word if it is not this already."[16] Later, "Scripture is recognized as the *Word of God by the fact that it is the Word of God.* This is what we are told by the doctrine of the witness of the Holy Spirit."[17] And finally, "The Bible is God's Word to the extent that God causes it to be His Word, to the extent that He speaks through it."[18]

So yes, Barth did say that the Bible becomes the Word of God. But understand this: Barth insists the Bible becomes the life-giving Word of God because he believed that is what it already is.[19]

---

[15]*CD* I/1, 304, emphasis added.

[16]Karl Barth, *The Göttingen Dogmatics,* trans. Hannelotte Reiffen (Grand Rapids: Eerdmans, 1991), 219.

[17]*CD* I/2, 537, emphasis added.

[18]*CD* I/1, 109.

[19]See also **Word of God** in chapter 4 below. For those who want to delve more deeply into Barth's account of Scripture "becoming" the Word of God, see Bruce L. McCormack, "The Being of Holy Scripture Is in Becoming: Karl Barth in Conversation with American Evangelical Criticism," in *Evangelicals & Scripture: Tradition, Authority and Hermeneutics,* ed. Vincent Bacote, Laura C. Miguélez, and Dennis L. Okholm (Downers Grove, IL: InterVarsity Press, 2004), 55-75.

I'm ready to start reading Barth. Where should I start?

The real problem with this question is like asking which food one should sample first from a grand buffet or international potluck: there are so many places to start—all good—that it depends on your own preferences and comfort zones. However, for the absolute Barth beginner, I usually recommend starting with a smaller work before launching into the *CD*. Barth's *Dogmatics in Outline*,[20] which is essentially a short phrase-by-phrase exposition of the Apostles' Creed, can be a great starting point. Or, start with his *Evangelical Theology: An Introduction*.[21] I have assigned this book to many of my students over the years, including college freshmen. Although there is some adjustment to his style needed, most find his reflections spiritually uplifting and challenging. Finally, I also recommend reading at least one of Barth's biblical expositions such as *Romans* (which is a challenge but extremely eye-opening) or *The Resurrection of the Dead*, which is an in-depth exposition of 1 Corinthians 15.

As for launching into the *CD*, I point you forward to chapter eight below, where you will find three different reading plans to get you into the breadth of Barth's "big books."

GURETZKI'S TOP THREE RECOMMENDED BARTH BOOKS (OTHER THAN THE *CD*)

1. *The Epistle to the Romans*
2. *Evangelical Theology: An Introduction*
3. *Dogmatics in Outline*

---

[20]Karl Barth, *Dogmatics in Outline* (New York: Harper Torchbooks, 1959).
[21]Karl Barth, *Evangelical Theology: An Introduction* (New York: Holt, Rinehart and Winston, 1963).

What will future generations identify as Barth's greatest theological contribution?

I realize that it doesn't really much matter what I say here because in one hundred years I will be either "dead-on" (and most likely dead) or "way out in left-field" (and most likely under a field). In any case, it won't much matter what I say here. But since you asked . . .

Following T. F. Torrance's lead, I believe that future historians will understand Karl Barth's relationship to twentieth-century theology as analogous to what Albert Einstein was to twentieth-century physics. This is because Barth sought to allow the object of inquiry, the self-revealing God, to increasingly dictate how theology is to be approached—mainly, to seek to understand God in ways appropriate to God's means of disclosing himself to humanity.[22] Taking Bruce McCormack's lead,[23] I believe that thematically Barth's doctrine of election will be most likely viewed as one of his most important and most unique contributions, particularly because Barth brought a perspective on election that views Jesus Christ as both the subject and object of election over against traditional Protestant and Reformed views that made election primarily about individual humans who are either

> **Jesus Christ, as he is attested for us in Holy Scripture, is the one Word of God which we have to hear and which we have to trust and obey in life and in death.**
>
> *The Barmen Declaration*

---

[22]Thomas F. Torrance, *Transformation and Convergence in the Frame of Knowledge: Explorations in the Interrelations of Scientific and Theological Enterprise* (Eugene, OR: Wipf & Stock Publishers, 1998), viii.

[23]Bruce McCormack, "Grace and Being: The Role of God's Gracious Election in Karl Barth's Theological Ontology," in *The Cambridge Companion to Karl Barth* (Cambridge, UK: Cambridge University Press, 2000), 92.

elect or damned. From no one else's lead but my own speculations, I predict that Barth will be an ongoing fountainhead source and inspiration for those who have sought to hitch the agenda of theology to the ever moving targets of being "culturally relevant," "philosophically astute," "politically pertinent," "apologetically persuasive," or even "religiously fulfilling" and who have found such agendas wanting because of how they so quickly become themselves respectively irrelevant, naive, pretentious, unconvincing, and unfulfilling. Barth's theology will persist not because he got it all right (who can get all things right but God alone?) but because it so consistently recenters our search for God in God's own search for us in the person of Jesus Christ whom we follow in life and in death. But of course, I leave open the (small) possibility that I may be wrong.

Who does Barth cite most often in his *Church Dogmatics*?

The names index for the *CD* reveals a sense of who Barth's primary theological dialogue partners were. Because he labored his whole life in the Reformed tradition, one would expect that John Calvin would be one of his favorite sources. Close, but not quite! Martin Luther actually edges out Calvin in sheer number of citations. Based on the names index, we find that Barth cites Luther 388 times and Calvin 340. Coming in at third place is Augustine with 254 citations. Beyond these top three, runners-up with at least 40 citations or more (in alphabetical order) were Anselm of Canterbury, Athanasius, John Gerhard, Johann Wolfgang von Goethe, George W. F. Hegel, David J. Hollaz, Irenaeus of Lyons, Immanuel Kant, Søren Kierkegaard, Philip Melanchton, Amandus Polanus, Johann Quenstedt, Albrecht Ritschl, Friedrich Schleiermacher, Tertullian, Thomas Aquinas, J. Wollebius, and Huldrych Zwingli.

FUN FACT

Barth's desk, at which most of the *CD* was written, is on display at Pittsburgh Theological Seminary. Barth was happy to receive a brand-new replacement desk in exchange for the old one that was shipped to the United States. He joked that he felt like a banker sitting behind his new desk. The seminary also has a reproduction of Matthias Grunewald's painting *The Crucifixion*, which hung above Barth's desk while he worked.

Did Barth believe in angels?

Yes. There are two convincing pieces of evidence that Barth believed in angels. First, he was convinced that they enjoyed watching him work on his *CD*. As he once mused,

> The angels laugh at old Karl. They laugh at him because he tries to grasp the truth about God in a book of Dogmatics. They laugh at the fact that volume follows volume and each one is thicker than the previous one. As they laugh, they say to one another, "Look! Here he comes now with his little pushcart full of volumes of the *Dogmatics*!"
>
> And they laugh about the men who write so much about Karl Barth instead of writing about the things he is trying to write about. Truly, the angels laugh.[24]

---

[24]Cited by Robert McAfee Brown, "Introduction," in Georges Casalis, *Portrait of Karl Barth* (Garden City, NY: Doubleday & Company, 1963), 3.

Figure 3.1. Barth's desk at Pittsburgh Theological Seminary

Ouch! (Of course, I'm not writing *that* much about him . . .)

Second, and much more seriously, Barth most certainly believed in angels because he wrote one of the most extensive doctrines of angels (and demons) in recent history, running some 169 pages in *CD* III/3. In short, Barth believed that angels had three basic functions: (1) they "precede the revelation and doing of [God's] will on earth as objective and authentic witnesses," (2) they are "faithful servants of God and man," and (3) they "victoriously ward off the opposing forms and forces of chaos."[25]

What kind of personality was Barth?

I obviously can't answer this question on the basis of firsthand acquaintance. However, based on the biographical details and stories

---

[25]*CD* III/3, 369.

we have, I think it is pretty safe to say that Barth enjoyed life, enjoyed his pipe, delighted in Mozart,[26] relished a good joke,[27] loved to converse,[28] loved to read, and loved to listen. In regard to the latter quality, Barth was like many genius personalities: he tended to be more curious about what others had to say, even though he was usually clearly the most powerful thinker in the room.

Barth was known for coming into sharp dispute even with his friends, sometimes to the point of relational estrangement. But that probably says more about his love for the gospel and for the truth of God being spoken than the all-too-human relational weaknesses that seemed often to beset him. Let there be no mistake: Karl Barth, the "twentieth-century father of the church" (who likely would recoil at the epithet), was a sinner like us all. In a letter near the end of his life, Barth modeled the stance that perhaps we need to emulate—a stance no doubt learned from Luther—when he said,

> I shall be made manifest before the judgment seat of Christ, in and with my whole 'being,' with all the real good and real evil that I have thought, said, and done, with all the bitterness that I have suffered and all the beauty that I have enjoyed. There I shall only be able to stand as the failure that I doubtless was in all things, but . . . by virtue of his promise, as a *peccator justus* ["justified sinner"]. And as that I shall be able to stand.[29]

---

[26]See Karl Barth, *Wolfgang Amadeus Mozart*, trans. Clarence K. Pott (Grand Rapids: Eerdmans, 1986, republished as Karl Barth, *Wolfgang Amadeus Mozart* (Eugene, OR: Wipf & Stock, 2003).

[27]Daniel Migliore, "Karl Barth: Theologian with a Sense of Humor," *The Princeton Seminary Bulletin* 7 (1986): 276-79.

[28]George Hunsinger, "Conversational Theology: The Wit and Wisdom of Karl Barth," *Toronto Journal of Theology* 17, no. 1 (2001): 119-32. See also Busch, *Karl Barth*, 463-64.

[29]Busch, *Karl Barth*, 499.

FUN FACT

Barth loved Mozart so much that he listened to a recording of his music almost every day. He once confessed: "If I ever get to heaven, I would first of all seek out Mozart and only then inquire after Augustine, St. Thomas, Luther, Calvin, and Schleiermacher." Source: Karl Barth, *Wolfgang Amadeus Mozart*, trans. Clarence K. Pott (Grand Rapids: Eerdmans, 1986), 16.

What were Barth's final words?

This can be answered in two ways. Although we cannot be certain about Barth's last uttered words (he died in his sleep on December 10, 1968), we do know that the night of his death he spoke in a late-night telephone conversation to his lifelong friend, Eduard Thurneysen. After discussing the uncertain world situation, Barth said, "But keep your chin up! Never mind! He [Christ] will reign!"[30]

As for his last written words, he had been continuing to write his *CD*, and on the night of his death, he had broken off in the middle of a sentence. He wrote,

The church would not be the church in conversion, proud and content with [?] its sense of the present hour, it would not listen to them [i.e., the apostles and prophets], or would do so only occasionally, loosely, and carelessly, or if it were to rob

---

[30]Busch, *Karl Barth*, 498.

what it has to learn from them of all its effect by [accepting] what they want to say to it . . ."[31]

Geoffrey Bromiley notes that it is fitting that Barth's last written sentence was incomplete. As he put it, Barth's "masterpiece, the *Church Dogmatics*, remained a magnificent but uncompleted fragment. The last word, after all, cannot be spoken by us."[32]

For Further Reading

Barth, Karl. *The Teaching of the Church Regarding Baptism*. London: SCM Press, 1948.

Barth, Karl. *Dogmatics in Outline*. New York: Harper Torchbooks, 1959.

Barth, Karl. *The Epistle to the Romans*. London: Oxford University Press, 1968.

Barth, Karl. *Evangelical Theology: An Introduction*. New York: Holt, Rinehart and Winston, 1963.

Dorrien, Gary. *The Barthian Revolt in Modern Theology: Theology Without Weapons*. Louisville, KY: Westminster John Knox Press, 2000.

Koebler, Renate. *In the Shadow of Karl Barth: Charlotte von Kirschbaum*. Eugene, OR: Wipf & Stock, 2014.

Mangina, Joseph L. *Karl Barth: Theologian of Christian Witness*. Louisville, KY: Westminster John Knox, 2004.

McCormack, Bruce L. *Karl Barth's Critically Realistic Dialectical Theology: Its Genesis and Development, 1909-1936*. Oxford: Clarendon Press, 1995.

Selinger, Suzanne. *Charlotte von Kirschbaum and Karl Barth: A Study in Biography and the History of Theology*. University Park, PA: Penn State Press, 1998.

---

[31]Karl Barth, *Final Testimonies*, ed. Eberhard Busch, trans. Geoffrey W. Bromiley (Eugene, OR: Wipf & Stock Publishers, 2003), 60.
[32]Ibid., 8.

Glossary of Concepts and People

The following glossary is a selection of concepts and persons most pertinent to better understanding Barth. There is obviously no way this glossary can deal with every difficult word or concept you will come across in Barth. For example, Barth spoke of "supralapsarianism" some ninety times in the *CD*, but his use of the term is not necessarily unique to himself. In such cases, you will simply need to look the word up in a theological dictionary. I have chosen instead to highlight only those concepts or words that Barth uses in a distinctive way. Further, I have chosen a very select group of persons that loom large in Barth's writings, particularly in his *CD*.

▶ ▶ ▶ **EXPLORER'S TIP**

For a reference of three hundred of the more common theological words, see Stanley J. Grenz, David Guretzki, and Cherith Fee Nordling, *Pocket Dictionary of Theological Terms* (Downers Grove, IL: IVP Academic, 1999). For a more complete list of over seven thousand theological words, see Donald K. McKim, *The Westminster Dictionary of Theological Terms,* 2nd ed. (Louisville, KY: Westminster John Knox Press, 2014).

Glossary

abolition (*Aufhebung*)

Barth's use of this word has caused significant confusion, particularly in paragraph seventeen of his *CD* I/2, titled, "The Revelation of God as the Abolition of Religion." The word "abolition" as used here is a translation of the notoriously difficult German word *Aufhebung*—a word with a long history of usage in German philosophy. *Aufhebung* can certainly mean "abolition" or "removal," but it can also mean "exaltation." Scholars in recent years have noted that the English translation leads to major misunderstandings of what Barth is trying to say. It can appear that he is trying to say that with the appearance of God's revelation human religion is abolished or done away with, leaving us with a religionless form of Christianity.[1] However, Barth intentionally wanted both sides of the "*Aufhebung* coin" to come out, arguing that revelation both abolishes human religion as a means of self-justification before God and also exalts and upholds religious practices when they align with what God has revealed of himself in Jesus Christ.

Ensminger helpfully clarifies how Barth understands the *Aufhebung* of religion: (1) Revelation will single out or highlight religion wherever it bears clear witness to Jesus, (2) revelation will restrain or abolish

> **EXPLORE FURTHER**
>
> For a retranslation of §17 and a helpful introduction to Barth's use of *Aufhebung*, see Karl Barth, *On Religion: The Revelation of God as the Sublimation of Religion*, translated and introduced by Garrett Green.

---

[1]Garrett Green, "Translator's Preface," in Karl Barth, *On Religion: The Revelation of God as the Sublimation of Religion*, trans. Garrett Green (London; New York: Bloomsbury T&T Clark, 2007), viii-ix. Green opts to translate *Aufhebung* as "sublimation" with the connotation of making religion sublime—better—even while recognizing the negation of religion inherent in the German term.

religion in order to bring about an understanding that it cannot by itself justify us before God, and (3) revelation will uphold and preserve religion wherever it properly and truly bears witness to Christ through its words and actions.[2] In short, Barth sees both a positive and negative outworking when revelation and religion come into contact. Barth, in other words, is not making an argument for abolishment of religion but sees the inadequacy of religion as a vehicle of God's revelation unless God so enables it to function this way (see **dialectic**).

abstract/concrete
Popularly, when a work is said to be "abstract" it usually means that it is difficult to understand or far removed from everyday reality, while "concrete" tends to mean something practical and usable. These everyday uses of the words *abstract* and *concrete* are not quite how Barth uses the terms.

For Barth, a theological concept or idea is said to be "abstract" when it is considered apart from how something appears in theological reality, particularly in the reality of the relationship of God to creation. For example, Barth would see the claim once made by scientist Carl Sagan, "The cosmos is all there is, all there ever was, and all there ever will be," as a theological abstraction.[3] This is because Sagan

▸ ▸ ▸ **EXPLORER'S TIP**

When scholars cite the original German text or make a point about the meaning of certain terms (as we will do throughout this chapter), it is good to understand that in German, all nouns, proper and regular, are capitalized (e.g., *Aufhebung, Bestimmung, Gemeinde,* etc.).

---

[2] Sven Ensminger, *Karl Barth's Theology as a Resource for a Christian Theology of Religions* (London; New York: Bloomsbury T&T Clark, 2014), 52.
[3] Carl Sagan, *Cosmos* (New York: Ballantine Books, 1985), 1.

makes a claim on the nature of the universe apart from its relationship to the God who created it. One might speak about the
universe as a "machine" or as "chaos" (two very different views of
the world) but again, both, theologically considered, would be "ab-
stractions" for Barth because they speak of the world isolated—
abstracted—from its reality as something created by God. Conversely, for Barth, a theological statement is concrete when it speaks
of a reality as it actually exists or as it actually has occurred in its
relationship to God and the world.

Two specific examples here will help. In Barth's discussion of anthropology (the doctrine of humanity) in *CD* III/2, he seeks to
answer the question of how the soul is related to the body. Barth is
emphatic that the Bible portrays the human as having both soul and
body. To speak about the soul or the body as if they can be considered in and of themselves is, for Barth, an abstraction that ignores
how humans actually exist in reality: as "always and in every relation
soulful, and always and in every relation bodily."[4] Conversely,
humans are concretely, as they exist as creatures of God, fully soul
and fully body before God. To speak of the human soul as a thing in
and of itself is an abstraction only. It's an idea that actually occurs
nowhere in humanity, that is,
there are no free-floating souls
that are not in some way united
to a body. It's an idea or concept
only and not an actual part of
created reality.

> The question of whether God can raise someone from the dead to immortal life *was* an abstract question until demonstrated defini- tively in what God actually *did* do in Jesus Christ.

Another example, much
more common with Barth, is
his repeated reference to the
person of Jesus Christ as the

"concrete form" in which God has and does definitively act toward creation. In this regard, Barth resists theological statements that speculate about what God *could* do in a given situation in favor of theological statements that are derived from what God *has done* in the history of his dealings with Israel and the church in the person of Jesus Christ. Thus, the question of whether God can raise someone from the dead to immortal life *was* an abstract question until demonstrated definitively in what God actually *did* do in Jesus Christ. Thus, the theological statement "God is the one who raises Jesus from the dead" is viewed, by Barth, as a concrete and theologically valid statement. It's a statement made on the basis of what God has actually done. The statement is concrete in the way that the statement "God is the one who can make a rock so big that he cannot lift it" is not—if for no other reason that we have no evidence that God has ever contemplated or attempted such a feat! The latter statement is an abstraction that has no connection to what God has historically revealed about himself or his relationship to the world.

analogy
At the risk of oversimplification, theologians through the ages have conceived of basically three ways to understand the relationship of theological assertions to the reality of God himself: Either (1) theological assertions are *univocal* (i.e., our words can, at least theoretically, perfectly align and correspond with divine reality as it really is), (2) theological assertions are *metaphorical* or *equivocal* (i.e., our words express human perceptions of what divine reality is like but are actually and ultimately incapable of capturing divine reality), or (3) theological assertions are *analogical* (i.e., our words are capable of representing something right and true about divine reality by way of comparison, even if in the end the two things being compared are ultimately more different than alike).

Some earlier interpretations of Barth's theological development (such as those by T. F. Torrance and Hans Urs von Balthasar) saw the earlier Barth as displaying a preference for "dialectical" (see **dialectic**) forms of speaking about God and the later Barth as increasingly preferring "analogical" forms of speaking. More recently there is a growing consensus that Barth never really left his dialectical form of thinking behind, even if he did rely increasingly on the use of analogy. Barth defined analogy as follows:

> In theology we can and should speak about similarity and therefore analogy when we find likeness and unlikeness between two quantities: a certain likeness which is compromised by a great unlikeness; or a certain unlikeness which is always relativised and qualified by a certain existent likeness. . . . In view of this likeness and unlikeness, unlikeness and likeness, we can and should speak of a similarity, a comparableness, and therefore an analogy between the divine activity and the human.[5]

> **Barth insists that the only point of contact between the Creator and the human creature is one that God himself has put in place in the person of Jesus Christ.**

Although discussions about Barth's concept and use of analogy can become extremely technical, beginning readers should note that Barth speaks of several types of analogy, two of which appear more frequently, and others of which appear only occasionally.[6]

---

[5]*CD* III/3, 102.

[6]For those who are ready to take the plunge on getting a handle on analogy in Barth, two of the best works are Keith L. Johnson, *Karl Barth and the Analogia Entis* (London; New York: Bloomsbury; T&T Clark, 2011); and Archie J. Spencer, *The Analogy of Faith: The Quest for God's Speakability* (Downers Grove, IL: IVP Academic, 2015). See also Gary W. Deddo, *Karl Barth's Theology of Relations: Trinitarian, Christological, and Human*

Barth addresses two forms of analogy most often: the analogy of being (*analogia entis*) and the analogy of faith (*analogia fidei*). However, he also speaks of the analogy of relationship (*analogia relationis*), the analogy of attributes (*analogia attributionis*), and the analogy of operations (*analogia operationis*).

Of all these forms of analogy, Barth is most adamantly opposed to the analogy of being (*analogia entis*) as a legitimate way of speaking about the relationship between God and humans. "We possess no analogy on the basis of which the nature and being of God as the Lord can be accessible to us."[7] Barth at one point even calls the analogy of being an "invention of the anti-christ" because it posits that humans can have knowledge of God on the basis of a commonly shared feature of "existence" (or "being") with God rather than on revelation per se.[8] This is going too far for Barth because of how strongly he wants to emphasize the utter difference between God and creaturely existence. Barth insists that the only point of contact between the Creator and the human creature is one that God himself has put in place in the person of Jesus Christ. As the one mediator between God and humanity (cf. 1 Tim 2:5), Jesus alone is the "point of contact" between God and the creatures he made in his image.

This does not mean that Barth rejects the use of analogy, but he insists that analogy, properly understood, can only

EXPLORE FURTHER
For more insight into Barth's rejection of the analogy of being, see the discussion of Barth's essay, "No!" written in response to Emil Brunner in chapter five below.

(New York: Peter Lang, 1999); and Battista Mondin, "Barth's Doctrine of Analogy of Faith," in *The Principle of Analogy in Protestant and Catholic Theology* (The Hague: Martinus Nijhoff, 1963), 147-73.

[7] *CD* II/1, 75.

[8] *CD* I/1, xiii.

speak of "partial correspondence and agreement" between God and humans (see **correspondence**).[9] Consequently, Barth speaks more positively about the analogy of faith (*analogia fidei*) as a means of speaking about God.[10] Barth appeals to Romans 12:6 where the apostle Paul speaks of a "proportion of faith" (Gk. *analogian tēs pisteōs*) that is "the likeness of the known in the knowing." For Barth, "this *analogia fidei* is also the point of the remarkable passages in Paul in which humanity's knowledge of God is inverted into our being known by God."[11] Or alternatively, the analogy of faith for Barth means that human words are capable of speaking *approximately* truthfully about God, not because the words are in some way inherently capable of carrying divine meaning but only because God in his grace "commandeers" those human words and causes them to reveal to the human real knowledge of God's own nature. As humans seek to speak of their knowledge of God, it is always faltering and incomplete; but God in his grace—as he apportions faith to human seekers after him—gives himself to be known in and through the words that we speak after him.[12]

To be sure, the concept of analogy as Barth understood it, and particularly the question of whether Barth finally did or did not completely reject the analogy of being throughout his career, is one of the enduring debates about Barth and his work. Yet analogy, and especially the analogy of faith, together with his commitment to dialectic, is in many respects fundamental to Barth's whole theological outlook.

---

[9]*CD* II/1, 225.

[10]So positive was Barth toward the so-called analogy of faith that Balthasar even suggested it was "the central theme of his theology." See Hans Urs von Balthasar, *The Theology of Karl Barth: Exposition and Interpretation* (San Francisco: Ignatius Press, 1992), 107.

[11]*CD* I/1, 243.

[12]For a fuller description of Barth's "analogy of faith," see David Guretzki, "Barth, Derrida and *Différance*: Is There a Difference?," *Didaskalia* 13 (2002): 54-61; and Gottlieb Söhngen, "The Analogy of Faith: Likeness to God from Faith Alone?," trans. Kenneth Oakes, *Pro Ecclesia* 21 no. 1 (2012): 61-64.

antecedence. *See* **correspondence**

Brunner, Emil (1889–1966)

Brunner was a Swiss theologian who was a friend and colleague of Barth's. In their earlier years, Brunner and Barth were often viewed as cofounders of the new "dialectical theology" but drifted theologically and relationally apart in the latter half of their lives. In particular, Barth resisted what he thought was Emil Brunner's belief that there was a permanent "point of contact" available to all humans as creatures created in the image of God. Barth rejected Brunner's concept because he thought that it led to a form of natural theology by which knowledge of God could be obtained through analysis of creation rather than on the self-disclosure or self-revelation of God.

Bultmann, Rudolf (1884-1976)

Bultmann was a German Lutheran professor of New Testament who worked at the University of Marburg from 1921 to 1951. Barth and Bultmann had both been part of the Confessing Church's resistance to Nazi socialism in the 1930s. Bultmann was in significant dialogue with the existentialist philosopher Martin Heidegger, and though he was influenced by Heidegger's categories, he insisted that he was not wholly captive to

EXPLORE FURTHER

For Bultmann's own clarification of the meaning of demythologization, see Rudolf Bultmann, *Jesus Christ and Mythology*. For a fascinating insight into the relationship between Barth and Bultmann, see Karl **Barth and Rudolf Bultmann,** *Karl Barth—Rudolf Bultmann Letters, 1922–1966.* For a succinct primer to Bultmann's thought, see David W. Congdon, *Rudolf Bultmann: A Companion to His Theology.*

existentialist categories. Although there are only thirty-eight entries to Bultmann in *CD*'s index volume, Barth himself admitted at the outset of volume IV that "I have found myself in an intensive, although for the most part quiet, debate with Rudolf Bultmann. His name is not mentioned often. But his subject is always present."[13] Barth held Bultmann in high regard for his insights but found he simply could not follow Bultmann's method of demythologizing as Barth understood it, and Barth (as was typical for him) tended to highlight the sharp differences he saw between them. Nevertheless, Barth acknowledges and uses many of Bultmann's own exegetical insights, especially in various places within the small-print sections.

church/community

Although Barth started his magnum opus, the *Church Dogmatics*, in the early 1930s, by the time he was writing the final volumes in the 1950s and early 1960s, Barth increasingly preferred to speak of the "community" (*Gemeinde*, which in German can mean both "community" and "congregation") rather than the typical word for church, *Kirche*. In his 1963 book, *Evangelical Theology*, Barth explains,

> The word "community" rather than "Church," is used advisedly, for from a theological point of view it is best to avoid the word "Church" as much as possible, if not altogether. At all events, this overshadowed and overburdened word should be immediately and consistently interpreted by the word "community."[14]

---

[13]*CD* IV/1, ix.

[14]Karl Barth, *Evangelical Theology: An Introduction* (New York: Holt, Rinehart and Winston, 1963), 37. The first section of this book is based on lectures that Barth gave to American audiences in his one and only visit to the United States in 1962. The lectures were originally released in German in 1962.

What is one to make of Barth's preference of the word *community* over *church*? There is wide recognition that Barth's later ecclesiology (i.e., theology of the church) is more akin to a free church understanding that places priority on the church's gathering, witnessing, and sending functions as true markers of the church rather than the more traditional Reformed emphasis, which insisted that right preaching and the right administration of the sacraments were the primary markers that defined the church. Although it's debatable whether Barth's mature theology can be truly said to represent a free church ecclesiology, Barth was most likely influenced at least in part by what he saw as the undue conflation of church and state in the European churches such that the church became too closely connected with the ideologies and agendas of the state (especially as evidenced in Germany in the 1930s and 1940s). Whatever the case, Barth increasingly preferred to use the term *community* over *church*. This was because he saw the word *church* as too closely associated with its institutional activity, structures, or polity rather than the words and activity of the people living out their confession of Jesus Christ in their everyday lives.

One of the plainest pieces of evidence of Barth's shift from speaking of the language of "church" to his preferred language of "community" can be seen in comparing the outlines of the first and fourth volumes of the *CD*. In *CD* I, Barth speaks often of the "church" (*Kirche*)—its proclamation, its theology, its Scriptures, its authority, and its mission. However, by the time he works out his massive fourth volume, Barth speaks extensively of the Holy Spirit's gathering (*CD* IV/1), upbuilding (*CD* IV/2), and sending (*CD* IV/3) of the "community" (*Gemeinde*).

To be clear, Barth already begins to define "community" by the time he works out his doctrine of election in *CD* II/2. There he defines community as "the human fellowship which in a particular way provisionally forms the natural and historical environment of the man Jesus Christ." Furthermore, he prefers the word community because "it covers the reality both of Israel and of the Church."[15]

correspondence (and antecedence)

Correspondence for Barth is a bidirectional concept that speaks first of God's relationship to human history and second of humanity's historical relationship to God. Both of these directions are related to a fundamental theological axiom, which for Barth is his belief that the triune God reveals himself in human history in such a way that there can be confidence that God *is* essentially as he reveals himself to be. That is, the manner in which God reveals himself in history *corresponds* to who God is eternally in himself apart from his relationship to history. Put negatively, God does not deceive us by presenting himself in a form other than he actually is. This does not mean that we fully *comprehend* who God is (no one can finally fully understand how God can be Trinity or what that really means), but it does mean that if God reveals himself as a triune God then indeed, God is triune independently of his revelation to us, or as Barth will often put it, *antecedently in himself.* Thus Barth can say, "According to the witness of Holy Scripture—in correspondence with his triune being, and as indicated by the biblical concept of eternity—God is historical even in himself, and much more so in his relationship to the reality which is distinct from himself."[16] Elsewhere, when Barth explains the notion of the Christian understanding that God is the Lord, he says, "[God] is this Lord, the 'Lord of all lords' (Deut. 10:17; 1 Tim. 6:15). He has this significance for us because it corresponds to what His being is 'antecedently in

---

[15]*CD* II/2, 196.
[16]*CD* IV/1, 112.

Himself.'"[17] Or again, "The content of revelation . . . of the divine lordship over our existence, refers us back to a corresponding inner possibility in God Himself."[18] Thus, in the first direction of correspondence, Barth sees God's revelation in human history corresponding to God's own unique "eternal history" antecedent in himself. Most important here is to understand that for Barth, God's eternal being always underlays his appearance in human history. Or to put it another way, *God becomes in history what he already is in eternity.*[19]

The second direction of correspondence for Barth is from humanity to God. In this direction, Barth understands that there is an appropriate response of words and deeds of humans to God, a response based on God's revelation of himself to us. Put simply, not any and every human response is appropriate to who God is in his reality. For Barth, this human correspondence to God relates to Barth's understanding of both theology and ethics. In theology, he is convinced that there is an appropriate kind of speech that properly corresponds to who God is: not everything we say about God necessarily corresponds with who God is. Thus, we speak of God as Father, Son, and Holy Spirit not arbitrarily, but because it appropriately corresponds (even if it is not identical to) who God reveals himself to be.

> **The content of revelation . . . of the divine lordship over our existence, refers us back to a corresponding inner possibility in God Himself.**
>
> *CD* I/1, 392

---

[17]*CD* I/1, 424.

[18]*CD* I/1, 392.

[19]Cf. the title of Jüngel's book: Eberhard Jüngel, *God's Being Is in Becoming: The Trinitarian Being of God in the Theology of Karl Barth*, trans. John Webster (Grand Rapids: Eerdmans, 2001).

Barth is convinced that there is an appropriate kind of speech that properly corresponds to who God is.

Likewise, in ethics, there is an appropriate kind of human action that corresponds to, or is appropriate for, who God is. As Barth explains, "The grace of God wills and creates the covenant between God and man. It therefore determines man to existence in this covenant. It determines him to be the partner of God. It therefore determines his action to correspondence, conformity, uniformity with God's action. . . . God's action is that He is gracious, and man in his action is committed to correspondence to this action."[20] Thus, when God commands something of us, "our obedience has to consist in an exact and concrete doing of this or that, as a human correspondence to the specific divine precept."[21]

To summarize, Barth's notion of correspondence is that on the one hand, God's appearance in history precisely corresponds to who he is in eternity, but on the other hand, the human correspondence in word and act to God's self-revelation is always approximate and asymmetrical, even if there are better and worse, more proper and less proper, ways in which humans ought to respond to the self-revealing God.

crisis (*krisis*, KRISIS)

Early in his writing career, Barth often made reference to the idea of "crisis"—a term Barth takes directly from the biblical Greek term *krisis*, which essentially means "judgment." Barth's use of crisis in

[20]*CD* II/2, 575-76.
[21]*CD* II/2, 744.

the *CD* harkens to his distinct employment of the word as he used it in his *Romans* commentary. Unlike the English word *crisis*, which has the sense of a particular problem that has arisen that needs to be averted lest disaster ensue, Barth uses the term *crisis* to denote the sharp divide or "infinite qualitative distinction"[22] that exists between God and creaturely existence. Beyond this basic sense, what does the term mean for Barth?

At one point in the Romans commentary, Barth insists that "Grace is the KRISIS from death to life." For him, this means that there can be "no tension or polarity," "no adjustment or equilibrium," and no "compromise" between grace and sin. Consequently, he insists, "the Gospel of Christ is a shattering disturbance, an assault which brings everything into question."[23] For Barth, then, KRISIS represents the absolute negation of all human efforts in light of the righteousness from God. Commenting on Romans 3:21, in which Paul announces a righteousness that comes apart from the law, Barth states, "We stand here before an irresistible and all-embracing dissolution of the world of time and things and men, before a penetrating and ultimate KRISIS, before the supremacy of a negation by which all existence is rolled up."[24]

> **We stand here before an irresistible and all-embracing dissolution of the world of time and things and men, before a penetrating and ultimate KRISIS, before the supremacy of a negation by which all existence is rolled up.**
>
> *The Epistle to the Romans*, 91

---

[22]Karl Barth, *The Epistle to the Romans* (London: Oxford University Press, 1968), 10.
[23]Ibid., 225.
[24]Ibid., 91.

In the *CD*, Barth continues to use the concept of crisis, though the translators have ceased representing it in the text as KRISIS per se. Although Barth has, to a degree, softened in what could be heard as an attack of "negativity" in *Romans*, he continues to uphold in the *CD* that God alone remains God and humans remain human; divinity and humanity remain wholly distinct.

▸ ▸ ▸ EXPLORER'S TIP

In Hoskyn's English translation of *The Epistle to the Romans*, whenever Barth uses the word *krisis* to refer to the biblical idea, the word was typeset using all caps: KRISIS. This aids English readers to keep in mind the sense of "conflict" or "judgment" that Barth was getting at rather than the sense of "emergency" that the English term connotes.

Whenever one comes across the language of crisis in the *CD*, the reader should take note that Barth is likely trying to uphold an important distinction that must not be overlooked or downplayed. So when Barth speaks of the crises that humans face—for example, a crisis in theological language,[25] a crisis in one's religious outlook,[26] or a crisis in a human's sinful deeds set against the sharp relief of God's own righteous acts[27]—he seeks to uphold and impress on the reader the sharp distinction and differentiation that exists eternally between God and creaturely existence. He is not, in other words, speaking of a current problem that might be overcome with sufficient human effort and ingenuity but of a reality that perpetually exists despite human efforts to counter it (see **dialectic**).

---

[25]*CD* I/1, 333.
[26]*CD* I/2, 297.
[27]*CD* IV/1, 528.

determination (*Bestimmung*)

On occasion, certain words are translated from the German into an English term that have unintended and sometimes unfortunate inappropriate connotations. One such word appears in *CD* II/2 in paragraph 35, section 3, "The Determination of the Elect" and in section 4, "The Determination of the Rejected."[28] The word "determination," of course, has a protracted history tied to the philosophical idea of "determinism" (as in "free will and determinism"). But the word translated in *CD* II/2 (§35.3-4) and *CD* III/2 (§45) as "determination" is the German word *Bestimmung*, which does not have the same connotations as "determined" in English. For Barth, the "determination" of the elect has to do with the "destiny" or "purpose" or "end" of the elect more so than being simply selected arbitrarily from among others who are "not determined."

Barth was known to borrow terms from others, and *Bestimmung* had a distinct meaning as used by philosopher G. W. F. Hegel, which included both the senses of "inner necessity" and "final goal or purpose."[29] The main point here is to understand that Barth is *not* talking about election as something that is solely "determined" by God in eternity past, but is something that constitutes the past, present, and future purpose of the one so elected or rejected. In other words, the determination of the elect is not about the logically necessary outworking of a predetermined decision of God about a human's eternal fate, but a statement about what it is that humans are created to be and how they are to live that out both in the present and in the future.

Deus dixit

A Latin phrase that means "God has spoken." Barth used the phrase in his first lectures on dogmatics while he was teaching at Göttingen

---

[28] *CD* II/2, 410-506.
[29] See Allegra de Laurentiis and Jeffrey Edwards, "Determination, Determinacy," *The Bloomsbury Companion to Hegel* (London; New York: Bloomsbury, 2013), 220-21.

to speak about the fundamental assumption that a theologian or preacher needs to make in order for dogmatics—theology—to be possible. If God has not first spoken, then any of our theological words are but speculation about an otherwise unknown and unrevealed God. The phrase itself in Latin is in the perfect tense and is thus difficult to translate into English. In its use, Barth means not only that at some time in the past God spoke but that in addition to speaking in the past, God continues to speak today in correspondence to what he has spoken before in Jesus Christ. A full translation that seeks to capture the import of *Deus dixit* as Barth used it would thus be "God has spoken and continues to speak in Jesus Christ as witnessed to in Scripture and the proclamation of the church" (see **Word of God**).

dialectic

One of the most important, and perhaps most difficult, concepts at play in Karl Barth's thought is that of *dialectic*. Prepare, therefore, for an essay masquerading as a glossary entry!

At its simplest, Barth understood dialectic as conversation or dialogue. To think dialectically, then, means to "think in such a way as there is dialogue. Two are needed for this. There must be two incompatible but inseparable partners in my thinking: a word and a counter word."[30] In this simplest of ideas, Barth understood theology as a conversation or a dialogue between God and humans, a conversation in which God has first spoken a word to which humans respond. The conversational aspect of theology as response to God is the most basic sense in which we can understand Barth as a dialectical theologian.

Yet Barth's concept of dialectic went much deeper than the basic idea that there is both a word and a counter-word. Dialectic in this

---

[30]Karl Barth, *The Göttingen Dogmatics*, trans. Hannelotte Reiffen (Grand Rapids: Eerdmans, 1991), 309-10.

deeper sense can be thought of along the lines of a both/and state of affairs or as a statement of two kinds of reality or states that appear to be mutually exclusive or even possibly contradictory. (For Barth, both the *state* and the *statement* are important dialectically— but we will come to this shortly). One can imagine a situation in which two radically different, if not seemingly contradictory, states of affairs appear to persist. Despite the apparent tension, we have no option but to make a statement as if both states of affairs are true. The dialectical "state" that appears to exist thus demands a dialectical "statement" to describe it.

An example of dialectic outside of theology in reality (and not merely as a set of logically contrary statements) is the nature of light. As scientists have studied the qualities of light over the last century, it has appeared that light acts as if it were a particle but also as if it were a wave. These two states appear to be contradictory: how can the same "thing" be both a particle and a wave? But every experimental indication is that light can only be fully understood to be both wave and particle.[31] Thus, *dialectically* we make a two-sided statement that in its natural state light is a wave *and* light is a particle, as strange as that may seem. We do not try to make the wave properties fit the particle properties or vice versa. Rather, we are forced to affirm both, even if we don't fully understand how this might be possible. So

> **Barth understood theology as a conversation or a dialogue between God and humans, a conversation in which God has first spoken a word to which humans respond.**

---

[31]To any physicists reading this, my apologies for what is most likely a dreadful oversimplification of one of the most important entities in the history of physics. For a legendary lay description of the nature of light as understood by modern physics, see Richard P. Feynman, *QED: The Strange Theory of Light and Matter* (Princeton, NJ: Princeton University Press, 1988).

dialectic, simply put, is affirming both sides of an otherwise seemingly irreconcilable or incomprehensible state of affairs where the evidence seems to point to both being true.

In the past couple of decades, Barth scholars have increasingly observed how thoroughly "dialectical" Barth was in his theology, even from the period when he was writing his commentary on Romans. In his careful study of the early theology of Barth, Bruce McCormack identifies at least four types of dialectic at play. For our purposes, however, we will discuss only the two types of dialectic that remained important in the *CD*: "Dialectic Method" and "Real Dialectic."

> **EXPLORE FURTHER**
> The four dialectics McCormack lists as at play in Barth's commentary on Romans (second edition) are (1) the Adam-Christ dialectic, (2) the Dialectic of Veiling and Unveiling, (3) the Dialectical Method, and (4) the Dialectic of Life. See McCormack, *Critically Realistic*, 266-74.

Dialectic Method. In his famous essay "The Word of God and the Task of Ministry," Barth makes the following threefold statement: "As ministers we ought to speak of God. We are human, however, and so we cannot speak of God. We ought therefore to recognize both *our obligation and our inability* and by that very recognition give God the glory."[32] Barth reminds his audience, filled with pastors, of the supremely important task they have been called to fulfill: "Man as man cries for God. He cries not for *a* truth, but for *truth;* not for *something* good but for *the* good; not for

---

[32]Karl Barth, "The Word of God and the Task of the Ministry," in *The Word of God and the Word of Man* (New York: Harper & Row, 1957), 183-217. For an updated translation, see Karl Barth, *The Word of God and Theology*, trans. Amy Marga (London; New York: Bloomsbury T&T Clark, 2011), 171-98. Although published as "The Word of God and the Task of the Ministry" in English, the German title for the lecture was "Das Wort Gottes als Aufgabe der Theologie" or "The Word of God as the Task of Theology."

answers but for the answer."[33] However, as the minister attempts to do well at this calling—to speak of God—he or she inevitably (sometimes more and sometimes less quickly) comes to realize that no amount of human words could ever capture or comprehend the majesty and mystery of God. Why? Because God alone is God—uncreated, glorious, and beyond comprehension—while we are but human, created, and to make matters worse, fallen. Consequently, the thing we know we *ought* to do we are *unable* to do (Cf. Is 6:5; Rom 7:18-19). We must speak of God yet we cannot speak of God! So what are we to do?

Barth's threefold answer gets at the heart of his dialectical method: (1) Recognize that as ministers and theologians, as followers of Christ, we are obligated to speak of God, and so we do; (2) confess the inadequacy of what we say about God, even as we are uttering it; and finally, (3) hope and pray that God in his mercy would use our faltering words by which some might hear God himself speaking to them. This is the dialectical method that Barth advocates.

Barth helpfully unfolds what the dialectical method looks like for theologians, beginning with the fundamental Christian confession that in Jesus Christ, the divine has taken on human flesh. From a dialectical perspective, what does this mean? Here an extended citation from Barth is well worth pondering:

> How now shall the necessary dependence of both sides of the truth [that the real God becomes a real human] upon this living Center be established? The genuine dialectician knows this Center cannot be apprehended or beheld, and he will not if he can help it allow himself into giving direct information about it, knowing that *all* such information, whether it be

---

[33]Ibid., 190.

positive or negative, is *not* really information. . . . On this narrow ridge of rock one can only walk: if he attempts to stand still, he will fall either to the right or to the left, but fall he must. There remains only to keep walking—an appalling performance for those who are not free from dizziness— looking *from one side to the other,* from positive to negative and from negative to positive.[34]

From there Barth goes on to give more examples that illuminate further his understanding of the dialectical method. On the one hand, we speak of the glory of God in creation, but then on the other hand immediately affirm that God has completely concealed himself from us in creation. Or we speak of the reality that humans are created in God's glorious image, only immediately to be reminded that humans have fallen from that same glory. Or Christians are reminded that in Christ they are master of all things and subject to nobody, only to be also reminded that Christians are a slave to all things and subject to everybody. All of these examples illustrate, for Barth, that ultimately, the questions and answers posed by human inquirers—by theologians and interpreters of Scripture—are themselves called into question by God himself. Consequently, Barth admits that following the dialectical method (or "dialectical way," as he sometimes calls it) of posing supposed contraries or tensions is no guarantee that God will speak. As Barth

> Dialectic is affirming both sides of an otherwise seemingly irreconcilable or incomprehensible state of affairs where the evidence seems to point to both being true.

---

[34]Ibid., 206-7.

puts it, "The possibility that God *himself* speaks when is spoken of, is not part of the dialectic way as such; it arises rather at the point where this way *comes to an end*."[35] But Barth also sees it, in the inferiority of other ways, that theologians and preachers must do their work.

Real Dialectic. Despite Barth's preference for the "dialectical way," he acknowledges that there are (and have been) nondialectical ways of doing theology. In his view, two main alternatives to a dialectical method are what he calls the way of dogmatism and the way of self-criticism. In dogmatism, the theologian seeks to speak very directly, by way of the Bible and by way of the settled dogmas of Christianity (Christology, Trinity, and so on), about who God is and what he has done and is doing. This, Barth notes, is

> **Barth believes dialectic better corresponds to the reality of the disjunction that exists between God and creation.**

the way of "orthodoxy," which seeks to conserve the longstanding teachings and assertions of the faith. Alternatively, Barth identifies, at the other end of the spectrum, the way of self-criticism or, better, the way of self-judgment or negation. He identifies this with the mystical elements of theology in the church in which the theologian explicitly and implicitly knows that all of her statements about God simply reveal that they and the one who utters them are wholly inadequate. Consequently, the way of mysticism, according to Barth, is when the human knows that the One who he or she really desires is *not* himself or herself.

---

[35]Ibid., 211.

To be fair, Barth sees strengths and weaknesses for both dogmatic and mystical methods of theology, but in the end he sees the
dialectical method as the preferred "third" option. But the question
is, *why* is the dialectical way to be preferred over the dogmatic or
mystical ways? To be sure, it is not, as Barth already mentioned,
because dialectic guarantees that the theologian will hear from God
better or have more accurate statements about God. Even the dia-
lectician realizes that unless God speaks, all her statements are still
wholly inadequate to capture the essence of God. Rather, Barth
prefers a dialectical method because he believes it better corresponds to the reality of the disjunction that exists between God and
creation—that is, that God is ever and eternally "over against" the
world and never to be confused with the world. God is, to use
Barth's (and Kierkegaard's) words from his *Romans* commentary,
"infinitely and qualitatively distinct" from the world.[36] God alone is
God, but the world itself owes its existence to this same God, even
while remaining completely and utterly different from God. In this
regard, the dialectic way of speaking corresponds to a "real dialectic"
(*Realdialektik*) that exists and persists in reality. As Barth puts it,

> The dialectic of the concepts God and man, or rather the real
> dialectic of the factors denoted by these concepts, has in the
> thought and speech of the biblical witnesses to revelation its
> exact correspondence in the dialectic of the concepts, or
> again in the real dialectic of the circles of being denoted by
> the concepts, of heaven and earth.[37]

For Barth, the dialectics variously represented as the dialectic of
eternity and time, of divine and human, of God being veiled in flesh
and unveiled in glory—are always asymmetrical, with the "God-
side" of the dialectic always having precedence and weight over the

---

[36]Barth, *Epistle to the Romans*, 10.
[37]*CD* III/3, 418.

"creation side" of the dialectic. Consequently, Barth prefers to speak "dialectically"—affirming and negating, negating and affirming—because it acknowledges that in reality God himself calls into question every affirmation we as finite, fallen humans can muster, and yet uses those same affirmations to bring about real knowledge about himself. Or to put it simply, as humans we are compelled to speak dialectically because we stand simultaneously affirmed and negated, negated and affirmed, by God himself.

Practically speaking, what does understanding Barth's dialectical method or dialectical way mean for reading the *CD?* Three basic things can be noted.

First, recognize that there are elements of dialectic woven through the entire fabric of the *CD,* even when Barth does not explicitly mention dialectic itself (though he often will). This means that careful readers will exercise due diligence in making statements about what Barth does or does not affirm. For in many instances, Barth will make some form of theological affirmation and expound on that affirmation at length, only to make some affirmation later in the same paragraph or volume, or even several volumes later, that appears to be in tension with the first. This can be one of the most frustrating aspects of reading Barth, and many have made errors of interpretation by relying too heavily on a single passage or volume without considering evidence elsewhere in the *CD.*

▸ ▸ ▸ **EXPLORER'S TIP**

Careful readers will exercise due diligence in making statements about what Barth does or does not affirm. In many instances, Barth will make some form of theological affirmation and expound on that affirmation at length, only to make some affirmation later in the same paragraph or volume, or even several volumes later, that appears to be in tension with the first.

Second, for Barth dialectical thinking generally is not the process of coming to a "higher" insight than might be arrived at by working with the two sides of the dialectic on their own. For example, juxtaposing the statements "Jesus is divine; Jesus is human" or "humans are male; humans are female," does not yield a higher statement into which the two terms of the dialectic can be resolved. To put it negatively, the dialectic of Jesus' divinity and his humanity, and the dialectic of male and female, is irreducible or properly basic. We cannot find a statement that adequately summarizes or synthesizes the two sides into a single statement. That means Barth's own theology generally resists being reduced to singular concepts.

Third, and perhaps most importantly, a proper understanding of the function of Barth's dialectics, of what they are intended to accomplish, will always yield *theological humility*. To return where we started on this discussion of dialectic, Barth fundamentally believes that the theologian, the pastor, the everyday Christian, is called on to speak about and of God but can't due to the finiteness and fallenness of humanity. Nevertheless, in obedience, Christians are called on to be witnesses to God's saving acts in Christ and so therefore must speak. But when we speak, dialectic reminds us that it is not our words or theological concepts that save but only God's own speaking to the human by God's Word and Spirit that ultimately matter. Consequently, we are compelled to speak of God, but we also do so with a dialectic of our own: humility and hope. We do so with humility that our words and theological concepts are wholly inadequate but with hope that God will take our words as an offering of worship to him and use those words in ways that reveal something of himself to others.

dogmatics

At least since the seventeenth century the word *dogmatics* has been used by Protestants to refer to a church's or theologian's

organized body of Christian teaching.[38] Today it is more common
to speak of *systematic theology,* and there are various examples
of theologians in past centuries who have attempted to write a
systematic account of Christian doctrine and have thus called
such an account a systematic theology. In this regard, Barth's *CD*
is, simply put, his attempt systematically to work out what he
understood the church had, and needed to, proclaim as
the gospel.

Barth's view of dogmatics, however, is somewhat different
than others' in their attempts to write a systematic theology, or
dogmatics, on at least three fronts. First, Barth tended to be wary
of the idea of a theological system that starts with a basic concept
or idea around which the entirety of a work of systematic theology is framed and built. Some might suggest a basic divine attribute such as love or sovereignty around which systematic theology is built, while others might hold that the authority or
inerrancy of Scripture is basic to theology. Some might think that
Barth himself has the doctrine of the Trinity as the basic systematic framework for his theology, but that is not technically
correct. This is because for Barth, only the Word of God itself—
God himself in his self-revelation, not just the concept of a Word
of God or a concept of revelation—is the proper basis for dogmatics. Indeed, according to Barth,

> the Word of God is understood as the centre and foundation
> of dogmatics and of Church proclamation, like a circle whose
> periphery forms the starting point for a limited number of
> lines which in dogmatics are to be drawn to a certain distance
> in all directions. . . . The fundamental lack of principle in the
> dogmatic method is clear from the fact that it does not
> proceed from the centre but from the periphery of the circle

---

[38] Alister E. McGrath, *The Genesis of Doctrine* (Oxford: Blackwell Publishers, 1990), 9.

or, metaphor apart, from self-positing and self-authenticating Word of God.[39]

Second, because Barth is writing his *CD* in the context of the modern European university, he is keenly aware of how those in "faculties of theology" would have been called on to justify the discipline as a scientific endeavor. This justification was usually found in the *prolegomena* (literally, "words before") of a systematic theology in which the theologian would clarify his methods and assumptions and seek rationally, and perhaps even scientifically, to give sufficient grounds or warrant for how to carry out the study. Barth himself includes a prolegomenon in his *CD* (and in his previous attempts at a dogmatics) but is ambivalent about the possibility of actually providing a convincing justification of dogmatics that would satisfy modern scientific expectations. Instead, Barth preferred to argue that Christian theology, although a science in its own right, is an independent science among other sciences because of the unique object of its inquiry: the living God. Consequently, Barth asserts that theology cannot be "proven" to be a science in principle but simply does what it does in obedience to God. Thus, Barth insists that "we should quietly insist on describing theology as a science" but also that "if theology allows itself to be called, or calls itself, a science, it cannot in so doing accept the obligation of submission to standards valid for other sciences."[40]

event (*Ereignis*)

The concept of event in Barth's theology is widespread, but two of the most common uses relate to his doctrine of revelation and his doctrine of the church. For Barth, the word *event* (German,

---

[39]*CD* I/2, 869.
[40]*CD* I/1, 10-11.

Ereignis) is meant to point to the ongoing, active, dynamic nature of God's ways of interacting with the world. In terms of the doctrine of revelation, Barth insists that revelation is better understood as a verb rather than a noun. That is, revelation is not a deposit of texts or knowledge (as in the Bible) but an *occurrence* or a *happening* in which a living human being comes into knowledge (or *encounter*) of God as a living God. Similarly, Barth will sometimes speak about the church as an *event* rather than a static organization or institution. The church "happens" continuously in the world as the people of God are empowered by God's Spirit to bear witness to the living and resurrected Lord Jesus Christ.

In cases where Barth speaks of revelation and the church as event, Barth means that "God's action can never be reduced to terms of this-worldly causality."[41] Thus, in regard to revelation, it is God who reveals himself to the human; revelation is *not* a consequence of either figuring it out or tracing the evidence for God's existence to a logical or historical conclusion. In regard to the church as event, the church is neither a work of humans, nor even a divinely and permanently instituted organization, but is always and ever a miracle of God's Spirit in the world. That is, God's Holy Spirit uses and works through people instrumentally to be witnesses to the reality of God's redemptive purposes enacted and embodied in the person of Jesus Christ. Event for Barth means that God is never

> **Revelation is not a deposit of texts or knowledge (as in the Bible) but an *occurrence* or a *happening* in which a living human being comes into knowledge (or *encounter*) of God as a living God.**

---

[41]Mangina, *Karl Barth*, 154.

a philosophical or theological or logical given but is always an active and real Actor and Agent in the world that can be anticipated and invoked and addressed but never boxed in or forced to act at human will or whim.[42]

history (*Historie* and *Geschichte*)

A common critique of Barth, especially in North America in the mid-twentieth century, was that he held to two different types of history, usually designated by two German terms the Barth used: *Historie* and *Geschichte*. Critics have sometimes suggested that Barth places certain events—like the virgin birth or the resurrection of Jesus—into a special category, *Geschichte*, which is understood by his critics as a "special history" outside of regular temporal history, *Historie*. But that misconstrues what Barth means by the terms.

It should be noted that Barth sometimes uses *Historie* and *Geschichte* as synonyms. However, when the terms aren't used synonymously, Ogletree defines them as follows:

> In Barth's usage, [*Geschichte*] refers to the reality of history christologically understood, history as determined by the sequence of encounters between God and man which has come to a decisive climax in the person of Jesus Christ. [*Historie*] designates the notion of history which is characteristic of modern historical thinking—history in the "historicist" sense.[43]

In other words, when Barth uses *Geschichte*, he generally refers to the unique events spoken of in Scripture regarding God's manner

---

[42]For the "event" nature of revelation in Barth, see Trevor Hart, "Revelation," in *The Cambridge Companion to Karl Barth*, ed. John Webster (Cambridge, UK: Cambridge University Press, 2000), 37-56. For the character of the church as "event," see Kimlyn J. Bender, *Karl Barth's Christological Ecclesiology* (Aldershot, UK: Ashgate, 2005), 168-73.

[43]Thomas W. Ogletree, *Christian Faith and History* (New York: Abingdon Press, 1965), 192.

of relating to the world, while *Historie* refers to the unfolding and subsequent recounting of everyday events that make up the totality of human history as understood apart from the world's relationship to its Creator. Thus, it's not that *Geschichte* and *Historie* are events that happen in different spheres, with one happening in time and space and the other happening in some kind of nontemporal sphere. Rather, *Geschichte* and *Historie* both describe events that happen in time and space, but *Geschichte* describes an event that cannot be traced back to generally accepted scientific or historical causes.

With this distinction in mind, *Historie* for Barth generally refers to those events investigated by modern scholars of history—events that took place at some point in the near or distant past. Barth does affirm that the event of the resurrection, the virgin birth, or even the creation of the heavens and the earth are *historical* inasmuch as they take place in a temporal time, but they are also events whose significance, and indeed, causation, are *beyond* investigation—and here Barth will often use *Geschichte*—using the regular tools that a historian would use. This is because these events are revelatory in nature and thus not simply events like other events; they have a special function of revealing something distinct about God himself and his actions toward humans. Thus, to use the example of the resurrection of Jesus, Barth insists that the resurrection takes place in our time and space—an actual historical date such as AD 30 can be assigned to it. But he also insists that as an event, the resurrection is not a historical event like any other. It cannot

> **Geschichte** and **Historie** both describe events that happen in time and space, but **Geschichte** describes an event that cannot be traced back to generally accepted scientific or historical causes.

be explained or explored by a historian by identifying the previous causes, precedents, or factors leading up to that event. Again, the resurrection of Jesus is not merely the coming to life again of a person (which might be able to be explained someday through attention to scientific or historical factors) but the resurrection of Jesus is the "happening" (see **event**) in history that vindicates the identity of Jesus as the Son of God, an event that cannot be explained through recourse to scientific and historical investigation.

The foregoing is not to suggest that Barth's conception of history is simple or uncomplicated. But readers must be aware primarily that Barth's concept of history is meant to address the "historicists" of his day (especially historians of Christianity such as Adolf von Harnack and Ernst Troeltsch) and their particular versions of history, which tended to restrict the concept of history to only those events that may be verified through critical investigation. In short, Barth understood the workings of God to take place always in and through human history but that not all of those workings, and certainly not their significance, can be discovered through historical, critical investigations.[44]

Luther, Martin (1483–1546)

Martin Luther, the universally acknowledged father of the Protestant Reformation, was arguably Karl Barth's favorite theologian. Even though Barth was a Reformed theologian and more closely aligned in that regard with John Calvin, Barth's affinity for Luther was evident in his **dialectic** method. Like Luther, who spoke of both *Deus absconditus* ("God hidden") and *Deus revelatus* ("God revealed"), Barth speaks often of the veiling and unveiling of God.

---

[44]For a classic, entertaining, and illuminating article on various theologians' view of history, Barth included, see Daniel L Migliore, "How Historical Is the Resurrection? A Dialogue," *Theology Today* 33, no. 1 (1976): 5-14.

Barth reveled in quoting Luther, often at length, and particularly many of his sermons. Readers should keep their eyes open for Barth's repeated use of the Lutheran phrase "in, with, and under," which was originally used to describe the way in which Christ was present in the sacramental elements but which Barth picked up and used in diverse ways throughout the *CD*. (See, for example, *CD* I/2, 447, 457; II/1, 16, 52; III/3, 19, 528; III/4, 334, 571, etc.)[45]

material/formal

Readers of Barth will undoubtedly come across his terminology of *material* and *formal* quite regularly in the *CD*. Although this is one set of terms that is not necessarily unique to Barth, it's one that bears clarifying sooner rather than later in one's study of Barth's works.

When Barth (and others in theological history, especially in the history of Protestant theology) uses the word *material* he means the very essence or reality of the thing being spoken of. On the other hand, the word *formal* means the way in which something appears structurally or in terms of the way something is stated, or the way in which something is received.

Perhaps one of the best ways to understand the difference between formal and material in Barth is in his understanding of authority. Barth understands that the church has in Holy Scripture a vital kind of authority to which it must turn in order to make decisions about its life, doctrine, and practices. However, in seeking to be obedient to Scripture, Barth would insist, the church is not seeking to be obedient to the Bible per se but to the authority to which the Bible itself points—God himself. In this way, the Bible is, for Barth, "not a material but a formal, not an absolute but a

---

[45]For an excellent overview of Barth's reliance on Luther, see George Hunsinger, "What Karl Barth Learned from Martin Luther," in *Disruptive Grace: Studies in the Theology of Karl Barth* (Grand Rapids: Eerdmans, 2000), 279-304.

relative [authority]."[46] In other words, the material authority of the church—the essential authority to which the church lives in obedience—is the triune God. But the formal authority under which the church labors and seeks to be obedient to God is found in the "form" of Holy Scripture. This is not to say that the material authority is the only real authority and that the formal authority of Scripture is somehow nonauthoritative. Rather, for Barth, the church needs to ever recognize that as it seeks to live in obedience to Scripture's authority it is doing so in order to live in obedience to the living God, not simply to a written code or law.

ministry (*Dienst*)

The word *ministry* as used in the English translation of the *CD* typically translates the German word *Dienst*. However, the word *Dienst* would be better translated into English as "service." For example, in *CD* IV/3.2, Barth spends considerable effort unpacking "The Service [*Dienst*] of the Community," which for Barth is meant to speak of the community's service both to God and to the world.[47] This service is revealed in various forms such as evangelization, preaching, mission, teaching, and the diaconate, which are themselves various expressions of the church's service to God and the world. These forms are not meant to suggest the structure of ordained or vocational ministry as service per se. Indeed, for Barth, these forms of service are for the whole church, not just for those in some form of vocational or ordained ministry.

nothingness (*Das Nichtige*)

In one of the more mind-bending sections of the *CD*, "§50 God and Nothingness," Barth develops the concept of those forces that have

---

[46]*CD* I/2, 586.
[47]*CD* IV/3.2, 830-901. The English translates the heading as "The Ministry of the Community."

a form of reality in the world and its history and that threaten and corrupt the good order of creation. Barth calls these forces provisionally the forces of "nothingness" (*Das Nichtige*). Nothingness is a notoriously difficult concept for theology, Barth contends, because it is a paradoxical reality that is simultaneously under the lordship of Christ but also "utterly distinct from both Creator and creation, the adversary with whom no compromise is possible."[48] He defines nothingness as "that which God does not will."[49] Barth's understanding of nothingness is probably the closest description in the entire *CD* of what is traditionally simply called "evil." Whatever one makes of Barth's description of nothingness or evil, it's apparent that he sought to give a rational account of this "thing" that he deemed to be ultimately "irrational." Nothingness, according to Barth, "is inexplicable, and can be affirmed only as that which is inherently inimical. . . . Being hostile before and against God, and also before and against His creature, it is outside the sphere of systematisation. It cannot even be viewed dialectically, let alone resolved."[50] In other words, nothing can be said about nothing that will make sense of its nothingness, even though nothing is something that is not nothing in creation. (I hope you have as much fun with that last sentence as I had writing it!)

> Nothingness is a notoriously difficult concept for theology, Barth contends, because it is a paradoxical reality that is simultaneously under the lordship of Christ but also "utterly distinct from both Creator and creation, the adversary with whom no compromise is possible."

---

[48]*CD* III/3, 302.
[49]*CD* III/3, 351.
[50]*CD* III/3, 354.

That said, Barth believed that even in its irrational, alien nature, nothingness "has already been judged, refuted and done away by the mercy of God revealed and active in Jesus Christ,"[51] even if it still will continue to resist and seek to bring chaos to the coming kingdom of God.

perfections

Theologians have long included in their work discussions about God's attributes—that is, descriptors that most appropriately portray God's essential nature. Barth is dissatisfied with the term *attributes* when applied to God because he believes that there is a danger that what is attributed of God could be confused with that which is attributed to a creature. Put negatively, Barth rejects the idea that, for example, "good" could be an attribute that both God and a creature can share in the same manner. "No one is good—except God alone" (Mk 10:18), he might say. The manner in which God is said to be *good* is qualitatively different than the way in which a creature might be *good*. Consequently, Barth prefers to speak of the *perfections* of God, which, strictly speaking, are unique to God alone. Barth insists that all of the so-called perfections of God are essential to his being, and thus, anything else that is said to be just, mighty, holy, merciful, and so on is so only by analogy to God (see **analogy**).

EXPLORE FURTHER

For Barth's discussion of his preference for the language of perfections, see *CD* II/1, 322-50. For a recent full-length treatment of Barth's doctrine of divine perfections, see Robert B. Price, *Letters of the Divine Word: The Perfections of God in Karl Barth's Church Dogmatics.*

---

[51]*CD* III/3, 366.

religion

In certain respects, Barth was on a warpath against religion ever since the time he wrote *The Epistle to the Romans* early in his career. There Barth set religion and revelation into sharp contrast such that he views all attempts by humans, including those who adhere to Christianity, as coming under God's judgment (see **crisis**). Accordingly Barth sees all such attempts as nothing less than forms of self-justification before God. Barth's perspective on the role of religion is nuanced to some degree by the time he writes his famous discussion on the "problem of religion" in the second half of his first volume of the *CD*. But even there, Barth continues to view religion as an element of opposition to God present in all human systems and ideologies. He defines religion as any human attempt to justify oneself before God, which God's own self-revelation works against, even to the point where Barth calls religion "unbelief" and God's revelation as the "abolition of religion."[52] (The word *abolition* here is problematic. See **abolition**.) Nevertheless,

> **EXPLORE FURTHER**
> The idea of "religionless Christianity" was explored, though never fully clarified, by one of Barth's most famous contemporaries, Dietrich Bonhoeffer, who sought to answer the question of whether Christ can become Lord of the religionless and whether there is such a thing as a religionless Christian. See Dietrich Bonhoeffer, "Letters to Karl Barth," in *A Testament to Freedom: The Essential Writings of Dietrich Bonhoeffer* (San Francisco: HarperSanFrancisco, 1995), 278-87; and Dietrich Bonhoeffer, *Letters & Papers from Prison*, Enlarged First Touchstone edition (New York: Touchstone, 1997), 280-82.

[52]*CD* I/2, 297.

Barth does not simply call for the abolishment of all religious practice—such an attempt would itself be a form of human self-justification. Even in the midst of the corruption of human religion, including the corruption of the religious practices of Christians, there is "true religion" by the grace of God, by which "God is really known and worshipped," and by which "there is a genuine activity of man as reconciled to God."[53] Religious acts, in other words, are all human, but by the Holy Spirit they can be used to accomplish God's holy purposes (see **analogy**).

Readers need to be cautious not to think that Barth is calling for a form of "religionless Christianity" that seeks to rid itself of all formal religious practice but for a Christianity that well understands the difference between its religious acts that are done in good faith in obedience to God versus the religious deeds that in themselves are viewed as acts by which we seek to be justified rightly before God. God may and can use the former acts but refuses to allow the latter in the accomplishment of his own mission and purposes.

revelation

For good reason, Barth has sometimes been called the "theologian of revelation." At least part of the reason for the epithet is that Barth so impressively revived an idea that had largely been overlooked among the many Protestant theologians of his day, mainly, that apart from God's own self-disclosure there is little, if anything, that can be known about God. As far back as his *Göttingen Dogmatics,* Barth insisted that the fundamental axiom of Christian theology is *Deus dixit,* "God has spoken" (see ***Deus dixit***), and that God has addressed humanity in such a way that real knowledge of him can be gained. As Barth put it, "God is completely inconceivable, concealed, and absent for those whom he does not address and who are not addressed by him. To receive revelation is to be addressed by God."[54]

---

[53]*CD* I/2, 344.
[54]Karl Barth, *Göttingen Dogmatics,* 58.

By the time Barth comes to write the *CD*, he remains as convinced as ever that revelation is utterly necessary for theology to carry out its task. Put negatively, without revelation there can be only speculation of what God is like, and no possibility of real knowledge. Consequently, Barth developed what has likely been one of the most

> God is completely inconceivable, concealed, and absent for those whom he does not address and who are not addressed by him. To receive revelation is to be addressed by God.
>
> *Göttingen Dogmatics,* 58

comprehensive doctrines of revelation ever attempted, a doctrine comprising the first two half-volumes of the *CD*, the doctrine of the Word of God. For Barth, revelation is not to be equated with the Bible, as sometimes Protestants are apt to do. Rather, revelation is the ongoing, living, personal disclosure of the reality of God's self to a human recipient—a revelation, to be sure, accomplished through Jesus Christ by the Holy Spirit and testified to in Scripture and in the proclamation (preaching) of the church. Most succinctly, for Barth revelation is God's own self-disclosure of himself through his Son Jesus as enabled by the Holy Spirit, and revelation "occurs" when humans come to know God as a living entity, not just when they come to know information about God.

It should be noted that Barth's idea of revelation stands somewhat in contrast to many other theologians in the Protestant traditions. For many Protestants prior to Barth, the concept of revelation pertained to the divine giving of inspired knowledge or propositions about God, most often understood as given in Scripture. However, as has been noted above, revelation for Barth is fundamentally about God's personal disclosure, or self-disclosure, to humans as a living Subject. For Barth, revelation is not simply about divinely revealed knowledge about God but about *real, relational* knowledge of God in his personal being.

Schleiermacher, Friedrich (1768–1834)

Friedrich Schleiermacher was a German theologian, New Testament scholar, and philosopher who is commonly tagged today as the "father of modern theology." One of his famous works was titled *On Religion: Speeches to Its Cultured Despisers*, in which he sought to restore credibility to the place of religion in a time when there appeared to be an increasing gap between the intelligentsia of his day (which was increasingly suspicious of religious authority) and the general populace (which was marked by continued widespread exercise of religious faith and practice).[55] Schleiermacher eventually wrote *The Christian Faith*, which was a new kind of "systematic theology" in which he gave central attention to humankind's religious sense of its "absolute dependence upon God."[56] For Schleiermacher, Christian doctrine is thus understood as

> **EXPLORE FURTHER**
>
> For Barth's interpretation of Schleiermacher's significance, see Karl Barth, *Protestant Theology in the Nineteenth Century*, 411-59. For Barth's lectures on Schleiermacher during his time at Göttingen, see Karl Barth, *The Theology of Schleiermacher: Lectures at Göttingen, Winter Semester of 1923-24*. For Barth's late reflections on Schleiermacher, see Karl Barth, "Concluding Unscientific Postscript on Schleiermacher" in *The Theology of Schleiermacher*.

---

[55]Friedrich Schleiermacher, *On Religion: Speeches to Its Cultured Despisers* (Louisville, KY: Westminster John Knox Press, 1994).

[56]Friedrich Schleiermacher, *The Christian Faith* (Edinburgh: T&T Clark, 1999).

the church's historic and ongoing understanding of God and the world in light of this sense of dependence.

In certain respects, Barth saw himself as engaged in a lifelong debate with Schleiermacher and tended (as he often did) to polarize his and Schleiermacher's positions. From the time of his early lectures on Schleiermacher during his time at Göttingen and through to his old age, Barth continued to have great respect for Schleiermacher's work. Barth's main concern, however, was that he perceived Schleiermacher as giving undue privilege to the place of the human spirit in theological reflection, and as a result, he saw Schleiermacher unwittingly replacing the Holy Spirit with the human spirit. Perhaps the slogan that represents Barth's primary concern about Schleiermacher's work was his assertion (with Schleiermacher clearly in view): "You cannot speak about God by speaking about man in a loud voice."[57]

Barth readers should note that many scholars today are seeking to bring increased clarity on Schleiermacher's own theological program, arguing that Barth's interpretation of Schleiermacher was somewhat lopsided and, sometimes, simply incorrect. But

EXPLORE FURTHER
Although already dated, the question of the relationship of Barth and Schleiermacher is helpfully explored in James O. Duke and Robert F. Streetman, eds., *Barth and Schleiermacher: Beyond the Impasse?* Two recent works noting closer readings of Barth and Schleiermacher include Robert J. Sherman, *The Shift to Modernity: Christ and the Doctrine of Creation in the Theologies of Schleiermacher and Barth;* and Matthias Gockel, *Barth and Schleiermacher on the Doctrine of Election: A Systematic-Theological Comparison.*

---

[57]Karl Barth, *The Word of God and the Word of Man* (New York: Harper & Row, 1957), 196.

his lopsided portrayal notwithstanding, Barth's interpretation of Schleiermacher is thorough and highly significant for understanding the modern history of theology.

Subject/Object (subjective/objective)

Barth commonly refers to the Subject and Object, or subjective and objective aspects of a topic. The Subject/Object distinction that Barth uses has its roots in Immanuel Kant's philosophy, or more at hand, the neo-Kantian philosophy that likely influenced the young Karl Barth.[58] For Kantianism, the terms *Subject* and *Object* refer generally to the *Knower* ("subject") and the *Thing Known* ("object"). This results in what is often called the "split" between the Knower (and her knowledge or perception of things outside herself) and the thing that is being perceived or known. Although in philosophy this created all kinds of epistemological problems (epistemology = the theory of how things are known), Barth picks up the terminology of Subject/Object and applies them to God and his self-revelation to humans.

Perhaps Barth's most famous application of Subject and Object is found in his doctrine of election. While Protestant doctrines of election had long acknowledged that Jesus was in some way the object of election (he was, after all, the Christ, the Messiah, the Anointed One, the Chosen One), Barth argues that Jesus Christ is both the Object and Subject of election. That is, Jesus of Nazareth is not only the one on whom ("Object") the action of election rests but also the one who is the acting agent ("Subject") of election.[59] In this regard, Barth insists that Jesus of Nazareth is not to be separated in some way from the second person of the Trinity. It is Jesus of Nazareth who is the electing God from all eternity, not just "God"

---

[58]For a helpful overview of the "Marburg Neo-Kantianism" at play in Barth's early thought, see Bruce L. McCormack, *Karl Barth's Critically Realistic Dialectical Theology: Its Genesis and Development, 1909-1936* (Oxford: Clarendon Press, 1995), 43-49.
[59]*CD* II/2, 157.

in general or even the prein-
carnate Son of God.

More generally, Barth is concerned throughout his *CD* to
show that God is both the
Subject and Object of God's
self-revelation. "God reveals
himself through himself"[60] is
the way in which Barth seeks to
show that God is both the ini-
tiator and agent of revelation
and is therefore both the subjective and objective elements
of revelation. More specifically,

> **Barth sees the Father as the one revealed, the Son as the one who ensures that revelation is *objectively* accomplished in history in the incarnation, and the Spirit as the one who ensures that the Son is *subjectively* acknowledged in the human recipient as the Son who reveals the Father.**

for Barth this works itself out in a trinitarian fashion whereby he
sees the Father as the one revealed, the Son as the one who ensures
that revelation is *objectively* accomplished in history in the incarnation, and the Spirit as the one who ensures that the Son is *subjec-
tively* acknowledged in the human recipient as the Son who reveals
the Father. Thus, when Barth talks about the objective and subjective aspects of revelation, he means that God both reveals
himself to be known in the person of Jesus Christ and ensures that
Jesus Christ can be really known by the human recipient for who
God really is—and this by the work of the Holy Spirit. In short, God
(Father) guarantees both the Objective (Son) and Subjective (Holy
Spirit) sides of revelation.

Word of God

It can be easy to assume, especially for Protestant readers, that
when Barth speaks of the Word of God, he is speaking of the Bible.

---

[60]*CD* I/1, 295.

However, it's more accurate to think of the "self-disclosure of God" whenever one comes across the phrase *Word of God* in the *CD*. God's Word is God's own speaking and unveiling of himself to human recipients. As such, the Word of God is not a static product of print per se but an ongoing event by which God speaks to humans. In his earliest dogmatic account, Barth argues that preaching and theology are possible and permitted only because God has spoken— *Deus dixit*. For Barth *Deus dixit* means "God speaking personally as the subject, God as the author, God not only giving authentic information about himself but himself speaking about himself."[61] Indeed, the idea of "God himself speaking about himself" is probably Barth's most succinct definition of what the Word of God is (see *Deus dixit*).

As one reads the *CD*, it becomes clear that according to Barth, there are three distinct forms by which the Word of God comes to humans: preaching, Scripture, and revelation.[62] Following his earlier assumption that *Deus dixit*—God has spoken—is the basis for all theology and preaching, Barth announces that "the Word of God in all its three forms is God's speech to man."[63]

That there are three forms of the Word of God does not mean that God speaks to humans in one form at one time and in another form at a different time. On the contrary, Barth argues that the three forms of God's Word are unified and must always be understood in relation to one another. In this regard, Barth maps out what he calls a "schedule of mutual relations" by which the three forms may be interrelated.

> The revealed Word of God we know only from the Scripture adopted by Church proclamation or the proclamation of the Church based on Scripture.

---

[61]Barth, *Göttingen Dogmatics*, 57.
[62]*CD* I/1, 88-124.
[63]*CD* I/1, 125.

The written Word of God we know only through the revelation which fulfills proclamation or through the proclamation fulfilled by revelation.

The preached Word of God we know only through the revelation attested in Scripture or the Scripture which attests revelation.[64]

Barth does not claim novelty in his understanding of God's Word in its unified threefold form; he traces the concept back especially to Martin Luther.[65] But more important than its provenance in earliest Protestant theology, Barth insists there is only one analogy by which to understand the interrelations of the threefold Word of God: the doctrine of the Trinity itself. Barth is so convinced of this that he can claim that "we can substitute for revelation, Scripture and proclamation the names of the divine Father, Son and Holy Spirit and *vice versa,* that in the one case as in the other we shall encounter the same basic determination and mutual relationships."[66] Interestingly, although Barth gives relatively brief exposition on the nature of the three forms of God's Word in *CD* I/1, he does not delve into depth until he first provides an outline of the doctrine of the Trinity—an exposition which he titles "Part I" of the doctrine of the Revelation of God.[67] Only then does he unpack Part II of his doctrine of revelation in which he explores the incarnation of Jesus, God's self-disclosure of himself in Jesus Christ,[68] and then Part III, the outpouring of the Holy Spirit,[69] in which he explores the Spirit's gifts of Holy Scripture[70] and proclamation (or preaching).[71]

---

[64]*CD* I/1, 121.

[65]*CD* I/1, 121-22.

[66]*CD* I/1, 121. For a more thorough examination of the relationship of the threefold Word of God and Barth's doctrine of the Trinity, see David Guretzki, *Karl Barth on the Filioque* (Burlington, VT: Ashgate, 2009), 84-90.

[67]*CD* I/1, 295-489.

[68]*CD* I/2, 1-202.

[69]*CD* I/2, 203-456.

[70]*CD* I/2, 457-742.

[71]*CD* I/2, 743-884.

For Further Reading

Barth, Karl. *On Religion: The Revelation of God as the Sublimation of Religion*. Translated and introduced by Garrett Green. New York: Bloomsbury T&T Clark, 2007.

———. *Protestant Theology in the Nineteenth Century*. Translated by John Bowden. New edition. London: SCM Press, 2001.

———. *The Theology of Schleiermacher: Lectures at Göttingen, Winter Semester of 1923-24*. Grand Rapids: Eerdmans, 1982.

Barth, Karl, and Rudolf Bultmann, *Karl Barth—Rudolf Bultmann Letters, 1922–1966*. Edited by Bernd Jaspert. Translated by Geoffrey W. Bromiley. Grand Rapids: Eerdmans, 1981.

Bonhoeffer, Dietrich. "Letters to Karl Barth." In *A Testament to Freedom: The Essential Writings of Dietrich Bonhoeffer*, 278-87. San Francisco: HarperSanFrancisco, 1995.

Bultmann, Rudolf. *Jesus Christ and Mythology*. New York: Charles Scribner's Sons, 1958.

Congdon, David W. *Rudolf Bultmann: A Companion to His Theology*. Eugene, OR: Wipf & Stock, 2015.

Duke, James O., and Robert F. Streetman, eds. *Barth and Schleiermacher: Beyond the Impasse?* Philadelphia: Fortress Press, 1988.

Gockel, Matthias. *Barth and Schleiermacher on the Doctrine of Election: A Systematic-Theological Comparison*. Oxford and New York: Oxford University Press, 2006.

Price, Robert B. *Letters of the Divine Word: The Perfections of God in Karl Barth's Church Dogmatics*. London: Bloomsbury T&T Clark, 2013.

Sherman, Robert J. *The Shift to Modernity: Christ and the Doctrine of Creation in the Theologies of Schleiermacher and Barth*. New York: Bloomsbury T&T Clark, 2005.

- 5 -

A Theological Pilgrimage

*A Ten-Stop Pre-CD Tour of
Barth's Theology*

The great Swiss Catholic interpreter and colleague of Barth, Hans Urs von Balthasar, once remarked that Barth's theology could be described as a *theologia viatorum* ("theology of travelers"), a "theology expressly designed . . . for a journeying People of God who are merely on their way to God but not [yet] there." Indeed, if there's any one thing that's refreshing about reading Barth it's that he spoke so confidently about God even while manifesting a humility that acknowledged he still had so much more to work out and to understand. But sometimes it's difficult to see where Barth is coming from and how he arrived at the confidence he displays in the *CD*. Consequently, I have found that becoming familiar with some of Barth's earlier works prior to the *CD* reveals some contours of his theological and intellectual journey. For me, it also makes reading the *CD* all the more richer knowing a bit of the historical context from which they have emerged.

Even though Barth is most well-known for his immense *CD*, he did not start writing it until his mid-forties. It's unfortunate that so many are unfamiliar with the riches of Barth's earlier works, many of which are often, in my opinion, far more interesting to read. In fact, there's a mountain of material (much of which still remains untranslated and unpublished) that Barth wrote long before he started writing the *CD* in 1932.

One of the features of Barth's pre-*CD* writings is the sheer variety of materials that he produced—from lectures, to sermons, to personal letters, to commentaries, to historical studies. Barth acknowledged that theologians were called on to carry out the task of doing what he called "regular dogmatics" (i.e., a systematic exposition of theological topics), but there were times when they were also called on to do what he called "irregular dogmatics." Barth admitted this was something "which all of us secretly do and which we ought to do boldly, especially if we are pastors."

This chapter seeks to give attention to some snippets of those "irregular dogmatics" that Barth produced prior to embarking on the *CD* in the latter half of his theological career. Here we will take a little tour of some of these works that represent Barth, "the theologian on the way" for "Christians on the way" to knowing and proclaiming God better.

In this pre-*CD* tour, I have highlighted ten works in the chronological order in which they were written, representing sources that should be easily obtained (most of which are still in print) even by readers who do not have ready access to a major theological library. I have also tried to represent the stylistic breadth of Barth's earlier writing. For some of the shorter works, you will be best served if the entire work is read in a single sitting. For longer pieces, I've selected at the outset an approximately twenty-five-page section from the selected work that will hopefully represent some of Barth's major theological concerns while highlighting his literary style.

"On the Sinking of the Titanic"[1] (1912)

Background. Barth started his career as a pastor, and for the first years much of his time was taken up in preparing sermons. After a brief pastoral charge at Geneva, Barth went to his solo charge at Safenwil, Switzerland, in 1911, where he spent almost eleven years as pastor.

The evening of April 14, 1912, was momentous in European history: news reached the continent that the mighty *Titanic* had sunk on its maiden voyage. On the Sunday following, Barth preached this sermon in which he reflects on what must have been the calamitous and troubling news of the marine tragedy. Clearly, the event had a far-reaching effect on the rank and file in the pews. Barth's sermon seeks to address the question "How could this have happened?"

What to watch for. Barth's text for the sermon is Psalm 103:15-17. For those accustomed to "expositional" sermons, Barth's sermon is sure to disappoint as he only marginally makes reference to the biblical text. However, Barth does emphasize what he believes are three basic points: (1) humans are helpless, (2) the tragedy should not have happened, and yet, (3) God's mercy came through even this disaster.

First, despite the impressive advances in technology being made in his time, with the *Titanic* standing as but one example of this advance, Barth makes the point that humanity is still small and helpless when set against the ways and will of God. As he puts it, "I . . . get the impression that in this disaster God has intended to show us once more that he is the boss."[2]

Second, Barth takes the opportunity to note that the disaster of the *Titanic*'s sinking did not have to happen. He cites approvingly

---

[1]Karl Barth, *The Word in This World: Two Sermons by Karl Barth* (Vancouver, BC: Regent College Publishing, 2007), 31-42.
[2]Ibid., 36.

a newspaper report in which the event was referred to as a "crime of capitalism" since it happened only because the company wanted to break a speed record of transporting people across the Atlantic Ocean. Consequently, the sinking of the mighty *Titanic* stood, for Barth, as a lesson of what happens when a few individuals compete with each other "at the expense of everyone else in a mad and foolish race for profits."[3] This sermonic application is noteworthy given that it was at Safenwil that Barth become vitally interested in matters of economics as it pertained to the social welfare of his generally working-class congregation. It was here in Safenwil that Barth became known as the "red pastor" because of his increased involvement with the socialist movement.[4] In this regard, the *Titanic* served for Barth as a relevant example of the capitalist spirit of profit set against the social well-being of everyday people.

> It is entirely God's will that the world's technology and machinery attain to higher degrees of perfection. For technology is nothing other than mastery of nature.... But I nevertheless get the impression that in this disaster God has intended to show us once more that he is the boss.
>
> "On the Sinking of the Titanic," 36

Third, Barth draws attention to "the other side of the matter," mainly, that "God's mercy . . . gives us hope in spite of sin and guilt."[5] So, for Barth, the sinking of the *Titanic* certainly points to the helplessness and sinfulness of humanity but also serves as an example of God acting mercifully through those on the ship who were reported to have acted nobly in the face of

---

[3]Ibid., 40.
[4]Timothy J. Gorringe, *Karl Barth: Against Hegemony* (New York: Oxford University Press, 1999), 30-32. See also Frank Jehle, *Ever Against the Stream: The Politics of Karl Barth, 1906–1968* (Grand Rapids: Eerdmans, 2002), 25-35.
[5]Barth, *Word in This World*, 41.

death to help those weaker than themselves. The moral lesson to be learned, Barth insists, is not only that the age is one marked by evil and godlessness but also that God's mercy "shone through the death and destruction of this disaster, so that we are grateful to be able to see it so plainly."[6]

This early sermon helps to give a picture of the theological liberalism that the young Barth had absorbed in his studies. The sermon was preached before the Great War when Europe was full of optimism. Technological expansion and moral altruism together were thought to be twins by which "kingdom of God and the brotherhood of man" could advance. Thus, in many respects, Barth's sermon simply reflects the tendency of his day to see theology as commentary on social and political issues, often with a rather optimistic tone. True, he alerts his hearers to the dangers of putting one's faith in an economic ideology or in the idea of technological progress—a message we still need to hear. But there is a glaring absence of reference to Jesus Christ, especially when measured against the later Barth. Indeed, Barth mentions "Christ" only once in the entire sermon and then only abstractly as a "force" coming into greater prominence in the modern world.[7] Though this is the same Barth who would so thoroughly disrupt the theological scene in years to come, this sermon, at this early point of his career, reveals a young pastor who, not surprisingly, sounds very much like his theologically liberal teachers.

Reading. Read through Barth's entire sermon, which is only eleven pages of text in the published version. You should also read Psalm 103, the basis for Barth's sermon.

---

[6]Ibid., 42.
[7]Ibid., 41.

"The [Strange] New World Within the Bible" (1917)[8]

Background. In the spring of 1917, Pastor Barth, who was still mostly unknown to the larger theological world, delivered a lecture in the church at Leutwil that would signal the beginnings of a major change in his theological perspective that had originated at the outset of the First World War in 1914. Barth's dismay over the ninety-three German intellectuals who supported the Kaiser's war policies, many of whom had been his own teachers, led him to wonder about the veracity of the theological framework he had received. After spending many hours and months in conversation with his friend Eduard Thurneysen, also a pastor who lived close by, Barth realized that they would need to "learn [their] theological ABC [*sic*] all over again, beginning by reading and interpreting the writing of the Old and New Testaments, more thoughtfully than before."[9] It was out of this reexamination of the message of the Bible that Barth's lecture on "The [Strange] New World Within the Bible" emerged.

> **EXPLORE FURTHER**
>
> The word *strange* was not in the original title of Barth's lecture (*Die Neue Welt in der Bibel*, "The New World in the Bible") but was included only in English translation. See Richard E. Burnett, *Karl Barth's Theological Exegesis* (Grand Rapids: Eerdmans, 2004), 74.

---

[8]Karl Barth, "The Strange New World Within the Bible," in *The Word of God and the Word of Man* (New York: Harper & Row, 1957), 28-50. The footnote to this lecture notes that Barth gave the lecture in autumn 1916, but Eberhard Busch indicates it was delivered February 6, 1917. See Busch, *Karl Barth: His Life from Letters and Autobiographical Texts* (Grand Rapids: Eerdmans, 1976), 101. Readers should also be aware that there is a new translation of this book now available, though many libraries will still have the older edition. All citations here are from the 1957 Harper & Row edition, but see Karl Barth, *The Word of God and Theology*, trans. Amy Marga (New York: Bloomsbury T&T Clark, 2011).

[9]Busch, *Karl Barth*, 97.

What to watch for. The driving question that drove Barth and
Thurneysen at this time was, "What is there within the Bible?"[10] Or
to put it in terms more up-to-date, "What is the Bible really all
about?" Barth admits that the Bible is full of history, morality, and
religion but that in the end, virtually anything can be found in the
Bible if one looks for it.[11] As Barth puts it,

> The Bible gives to every man and to every era such answers
> to their questions as they deserve. We shall always find in it
> as much as we seek and no more: high and divine content if it
> is high and divine content that we seek; transitory and "his-
> torical" content, if it is transitory and "historical" content that
> we seek—nothing whatever, if it is nothing whatever that we
> seek. The hungry are satisfied by it, and to the satisfied it is
> surfeiting before they have opened it. The question, What is
> within the Bible? has a mortifying way of converting itself into
> the question, Well, what are you looking for, and who are you,
> pray, who make bold to look?[12]

The problem, of course, is that even if all these things may be found
for the one who looks, does this get at what the Bible is really all
about? Barth was not convinced. What then is in the Bible?

> It is not the right human thoughts about God which form
> the content of the Bible, but the right divine thoughts
> about men. The Bible tells us not how we should talk with
> God but what he says to us; not how we find the way to him,
> but how has sought and found the way to us; not the right
> relation in which we must place ourselves to him, but the
> covenant which he has made with all who are Abraham's

---

[10]Barth, "Strange New World," 31.
[11]Ibid., 35-37, 37-40, 41-43.
[12]Ibid., 32.

spiritual children and which he has sealed once and for all in Jesus Christ.[13]

This essay represented what some scholars call Barth's "first conversion"—a conversion away from an understanding of the Bible that focused primarily on its original historical, cultural, and literary contexts—an understanding of the Bible that Barth had learned in his university education. But it is important to note that Barth's so-called conversion does not lead him to negate the reality of the Bible's historical situatedness. It is not that Barth disputed that history, morality, and religion could be found in the Bible but that to read it *only* with those expectations is to see only the human standpoint and to miss the very "standpoint of God."[14] Barth discovered that the Bible was where the church could go to hear God's own word to humans. In short, Barth begins to argue here—in ways he had not yet done up to this point—that there is "revelation in the Bible and not religion only."[15] What is in the Bible? "We have found in the Bible a new world, God, God's sovereignty, God's glory, God's incomprehensible love. Not the history of man but the history of God! . . . Not human standpoints but the standpoint of God."[16]

This essay is significant because it is a piece of literary, theological, and biographical evidence for major shifts in Barth's thinking—shifts that marked him as an independent

> **It is not the right human thoughts about God which form the content of the Bible, but the right divine thoughts about men.**
>
> "The Strange New World Within the Bible," 43

---

[13]Ibid., 43.
[14]Ibid., 44.
[15]Ibid.
[16]Ibid., 45.

and revolutionary theologian. At the same time it demonstrates that Barth's shift of thinking was a result of renewed attention to the message and content of the Bible.

Reading. Read the entire essay (twenty-three pages). Go ahead. It's good for you.

The Epistle to the Romans (1919, 1922)[17]

Background. Barth's lecture "The Strange New World Within the Bible" was delivered at a time when Barth was working on a much larger piece that he never intended to be published—mainly, his commentary on Paul's epistle to the Romans. Starting in 1916, Barth had filled notebook after notebook of commentary on Romans, a practice he continued for the next two years. By 1918, Barth had finished a draft of the commentary and decided to see if it could be published. Although dated 1919, the commentary was published in December 1918. Only one thousand copies were printed, and only when distribution spread beyond his native Switzerland did Barth's commentary begin to be noticed. After some positive and stingingly negative reviews, Barth decided that the commentary needed to be reworked—which he did in 1920—and in 1921.

What to watch for. English readers do not (yet) have a translation of the first edition of Barth's *Römerbrief* but rather only the second, greatly revised edition. (There were

> Religion spells disruption, discord, and the absence of peace. A man at one with himself is a man still unacquainted with the great problem of his union with God.
>
> **Barth,** commenting on Romans 7:21-23 (266)

---

[17]Karl Barth, *The Epistle to the Romans* (London: Oxford University Press, 1968).

actually six editions, but editions three through six are minor revisions of the radically revised second edition.) For those accustomed to reading biblical commentaries, Barth's *Romans* takes some getting used to. Although he proceeds customarily straight through the text of Paul's epistle, he tends to be far less concerned about Greek grammar or semantics and far more concerned about trying to "see through" the text to see what Paul saw. To put it another way, Barth was less concerned to get at what Paul *meant* and much more concerned to see the subject matter to which Paul himself was pointing.[18]

It's easy to be put off by Barth's *Romans*, especially if one is expecting the typical matters germane to a commentary. Barth's written style is full of idiosyncrasies. The commentary is peppered with exclamation points and dashed phrases; references to Kierkegaard and Nietzsche interspersed with references to Abraham, Isaiah, and Psalms; repetition and broken-off sentences; and constant use of terms like "KRISIS"[19] or "contradiction." Not surprisingly, the text is also littered with military and war allusions.

Furthermore, *Romans* is difficult to characterize because though it presents itself in form as a commentary, in genre it reads much more like a theological manifesto, somewhat more akin to a long version of Martin Luther King Jr.'s "I Have a Dream" speech than a

> **EXPLORE FURTHER**
>
> For an analysis of Barth's rhetorical strategies, particularly in his *Romans* period, see Stephen H. Webb, *Re-Figuring Theology: The Rhetoric of Karl Barth*.

---

[18]See Richard E. Burnett, *Karl Barth's Theological Exegesis* (Grand Rapids: Eerdmans, 2004).

[19]See **crisis** in chapter 4 above.

scholarly treatise on Romans. But rather than pronouncing his vision of the future, Barth's message was simple yet thundered in the ears of those who heard it: "Let God be God!" Or more fully, "The Gospel is not a religious message to inform mankind of their divinity or to tell them how they may become divine . . . [nor] is it one thing in the midst of other things. . . . Rather, it is the clear and objective perception of what eye hath not seen nor ear heard."[20]

It was *Romans* that launched the otherwise unknown pastor laboring in the ecclesial pasture of Safenwil into the more rarified atmosphere of academia, and it was this work that Karl Adam described as landing like a "bombshell in the playground of the theologians."[21] Not only does *Romans* reveal something of the theological flavor of the early Barth, but it also challenges readers afresh today with the thunderous message that Barth himself claimed to have heard the apostle preaching.[22]

Reading. First, read Barth's preface to the first and second editions (pp. 1-15). Follow this up by reading pages 362-74 where Barth speaks about the "KRISIS of Knowledge"—an exposition of Romans 9:30–10:2.

EXPLORE FURTHER
For an excellent analysis of Barth's interpretative strategies in *Romans,* see Richard E. Burnett, *Karl Barth's Theological Exegesis.*

---

[20]Barth, *Epistle to the Romans,* 28.

[21]Karl Adam, *Das Hochland,* June 1926, as referenced in J. McConnachie, "The Teaching of Karl Barth," *Hibbert Journal* 25 (1926–1927): 385.

[22]For one of the better theological introductions to the significance of Barth's commentary on Romans, see John Webster, "Karl Barth," in *Reading Romans Through the Centuries: From the Early Church to Karl Barth,* ed. Jeffrey P. Greenman and Timothy Larsen (Grand Rapids: Baker Books, 2005), 205-23.

"The Word of God and the Task of the Ministry" (1922)[23]

Background. Upon publication of *Romans,* Barth received an invitation to take up a post as honorary chair of Reformed theology at the German university of Göttingen whose faculty members, for the most part, were Lutheran in orientation. Barth took up the post in October 1921 and reminisced that his first semesters were extremely stressful for him as he sought to transition away from the parish to academic life. Nevertheless, the new post allowed him to get caught up in his own understanding of the history of Reformed theology—a field that Barth felt woefully underprepared to teach. Even though Barth was an "honorary" professor whose lectures and classes were not required for the students, his classrooms soon became full of eager Lutheran students coming to hear the lectures in Reformed theology, a situation that quickly caused tension among some of the senior faculty.

About one year after his arrival at Göttingen, Barth was invited to address a group called "Friends of *Christian World*"—an association of supporters of the journal *Christliche Welt* ("Christian World"), which Barth himself had served as an editorial assistant in his own student days in 1908.[24] It was on this occasion that Barth delivered his famous lecture titled "The Word of God and the Task of the Ministry."

What to watch for. In the lecture, Barth addresses what for him had been an all-too-familiar sentiment that he himself had faced as a preacher just months previously—that is, how it is possible as a mere human to say a word supposedly about and on behalf of God. Barth's thesis is as follows: "As ministers we ought to speak of God.

---

[23]Karl Barth, "The Word of God and the Task of the Ministry," in *The Word of God and the Word of Man* (New York: Harper & Row, 1957), 183-217. The original title of the lecture was actually "The Word of God as the Task of Theology."

[24]Busch, *Karl Barth*, 46.

We are human, however, and so we cannot speak of God. We ought therefore to recognize both *our obligation and our inability* and by that very recognition give God the glory."[25]

This essay is significant, according to Barth's biographer, Eberhard Busch, as "probably the most pregnant expression of what was then called 'dialectical theology.'"[26] According to Barth, when faced with the dilemma as outlined—how can a mere human preach God's Word?—there are really only three directions one can take. Barth identifies these three ways as the way of dogmatism, the way of self-criticism, and the way of dialectic. He admits that these ways are "distinguishable from one another, we may note, only in theory" and that "no real religious teacher has ever lived who took only one of them," and he cites Luther as an example of one who at various points took all three ways.[27] So what do these three ways represent?

Dogmatism. The way of dogmatism relies on, more or less, the Bible and the received doctrines (or dogmas) and creeds of the church in its familiar orthodox ideas about Christ, the Trinity, salvation, and eschatology. The minister or theologian in this mode returns often with a "taste of objectivity" and reiterates the teachings about God that have become familiar to Christian faith, so much so that it eventually becomes difficult to

> When a man becomes really aware of the incompleteness of all human work, the only possible response he can make to this awareness is to go eagerly to work—but when we have done everything we are responsible for, we shall have to say we are unprofitable servants.
>
> "The Word of God and the Task of the Ministry," 207-8

---

[25]Barth, "The Word of God and the Task of the Ministry," 186.
[26]Busch, *Karl Barth*, 140.
[27]Barth, "The Word of God and the Task of the Ministry," 200.

think otherwise. Although Barth admits with Luther that the way of dogmatism is a better route than the way of historical reconstruction or criticism, he also points out how easily a person can confuse *orthodoxy* with God, and how easy it can be to speak of the doctrine of God rather than of the living God himself!

Self-criticism. On the other hand, there are also those who, upon receiving a sense of the reality of God himself, become aware of, in contrast, their frail humanity. It is on this recognition of the utter "otherness" of God's perfect being that the human is "bidden as a man to die, to surrender all his uniqueness, his self-hood, his ego-hood."[28] Barth calls this the way of mysticism, "a way that must be reckoned with!" To be sure, Barth insists, better to be seriously attacked by God, to be so overwhelmed by God that there is nothing left of the human. Mysticism—the way of self-*criticism,* or more accurately, the way of self-negation[29]—is better than assuming that somehow the human mind has captured God! Yet mysticism, too, leaves the inquirer with no positive knowledge of God—only the negations of the mystic who can do nothing more than utter, "Who can know of God?" and "I am not God."

Dialectic. In light of the inadequacies of the dogmatic and self-critical ways, Barth proposes a third—the way of dialectic. This way, Barth argues, simultaneously "undertakes seriously and positively to develop the idea of God on the one hand and the criticism of man and all things human on the other; but they are not now considered independently but are both referred constantly to their common presupposition, to the living truth."[30] For Barth, this meant that the theologian/preacher was called on constantly "to interpret the Yes and the No and the No by the Yes without delaying more than a

---

[28]Ibid., 203.
[29]See **crisis** in chapter 4 above.
[30]Barth, "The Word of God and the Task of the Ministry," 206.

moment in either a fixed Yes *or* a fixed No."[31] In other words, the only way to speak of God is simultaneously to acknowledge that we *must*, and that we *can't*, but that we *must anyways*. It is a process of constantly going back and forth between the possibility and impossibility without pausing too long on either side of the "dialectic."[32]

▸ ▸ ▸ **EXPLORER'S TIP**

Göttingen Dogmatics was originally published as *Unterricht in der christlichen Religion*. The title of Barth's lectures was "Instruction in the Christian Religion," an unmistakable echo of John Calvin's *Institutes of the Christian Religion*.

Lest Barth leave his hearers in a state of despair, he concludes with his third sentence, which affirms that though we ought to speak of God and though we cannot, we nevertheless are called, as preachers and teachers, to do nothing less than to give God the glory. Indeed, to give glory to God alone, *soli Deo gloria,* is the only conclusion to be offered to the "necessary and impossible task of the minister."[33]

Readers who struggle with the concept of Barth's dialectical method of theology cannot afford to overlook this seminal essay. It presents in the earliest and most formative stages the emerging "dialecticism" of Karl Barth, the lifelong dialectical theologian.

Reading. The entire essay is only thirty-six pages in length. Go ahead and read the whole thing.

Göttingen Dogmatics (1924)[34]

Background. Owing to Barth's self-confessed lack of confidence in carrying out his task as a professor of Reformed dogmatics,

---

[31]Ibid., 207.
[32]See **dialectic** in chapter 4 above.
[33]Barth, "The Word of God and the Task of the Ministry," 213.
[34]Karl Barth, *Göttingen Dogmatics*, trans. Hannelotte Reiffen (Grand Rapids: Eerdmans, 1991).

he took up the challenge of devoting his first years at Göttingen to tutoring himself and his students in the history of Reformed theology. He lectured on the Heidelberg Catechism, John Calvin, Huldrych Zwingli, the Reformed confessions, and finally, Friedrich Schleiermacher. Coupled with his historical study, Barth did a series of exegetical lectures on Ephesians, James, 1 Corinthians, and 1 John because he was convinced that Scripture was central to an evangelical dogmatics and that exposition of Scripture was key to understanding the Reformers.[35] As a constant companion on this journey, Barth leaned heavily on Heinrich Heppe's *Reformed Dogmatics*,[36] basically his early tutor in the history of Reformed theology.

Starting in summer 1924, Barth finally began to lecture on dogmatic themes. English readers now have access to these lectures in the first volume appropriately titled *The Göttingen Dogmatics* (*GD*). Here we are given insights into Barth's first attempts at a formal dogmatics.

EXPLORE FURTHER

For an excellent introduction to the *GD*, see Daniel I. Migliore, "Karl Barth's First Lectures in Dogmatics: Instruction in the Christian Religion," in *The Göttingen Dogmatics: Instruction in the Christian Religion*.

What to watch for. After a relatively brief introductory section on "The Word of God as the Problem of Dogmatics," Barth's first lectures in dogmatics pick up from where he had found himself in the recent past: as a preacher. Indeed, Barth insists that the task of dogmatics begins with the assumption of the Christian

---

[35]Karl Barth, "Karl Barth's Foreword," in *Reformed Dogmatics* (Grand Rapids: Baker Book House, n.d.), v.

[36]Heinrich Heppe, *Reformed Dogmatics*, ed. Ernst Bizer, trans. G. T. Thomson (Eugene, OR: Wipf & Stock Publishers, 2008).

speaking. Reflection on preaching—on the extent to which we can (or cannot) speak of God—is the point of dogmatics.[37]

But Barth does not settle with the assumption that the only reason Christians engage in theological reflection is that we sometimes, even often, speak of God. Rather, Barth argues that the reason that Christians can "dare to speak about God" is only because God himself has first spoken to us. It is here that Barth takes up the phrase *Deus dixit* ("God has spoken") as the fundamental assumption that drives the work of Christian theology. As he puts it, "The prophets and apostles could no more talk about God than we can. Their witness, then, is *Deus dixit*, God has spoken. Scripture is the basis of preaching, but it, too, has a basis in a third thing even further back. It is the witness to revelation." And for Barth, it is this witness to the original revelation of God, of God's disclosure of himself to the prophets and apostles of old, that gives preachers today "the permission and command to speak of God."[38]

The remainder of Barth's opening lectures in dogmatics was paradigmatic for the eventual shape of his mature *CD.* He posits that God is the speaking subject to which dogmatic work must respond and that therefore, the starting point of a truly Christian theology of God must be with the doctrine of the Trinity, only after which he is able to deal with issues such as authority, Scripture, and even the doctrine of election. It was this basic shape, with notable deletions

> There is no lack of good preachers and sermons, but a lack of sermons that are meant to be God's Word and are received as such—a lack of *qualified* preaching.
>
> *Göttingen Dogmatics,* 31

---

[37]Barth, *Göttingen Dogmatics,* 30.
[38]Ibid., 56.

and expansions later on, that is reflected in the outline of the mature *CD*. Although Barth later admitted that his first attempts at dogmatics were still too indebted to the categories of philosophical existentialism,[39] the *GD* undoubtedly stands as the fundamental starting point of his own formal dogmatic efforts. Readers who take the time to delve into the *GD* will most certainly sense the young theologian's energetic zeal in carrying out his task, including more glimpses than anywhere else of the humor and twinkle in his eye that evidenced that Barth was truly enjoying the journey.

Reading. It's extremely difficult to limit ourselves to a short selection from the *Göttingen Dogmatics*, but I believe that Barth's discussion of *Deus dixit* represents a fundamental, axiomatic starting point for the entirety of Barth's theological contribution. Go ahead and read pages 45-63. If you still have appetite and time for more, then I recommend moving on to an earlier short section in which Barth reflects on the nature of the Word of God (pp. 14-18)—a reflection that funds Barth's later, much more developed concept of the threefold form of the Word of God as manifest in the first half-volume of the *CD*.

Witness to the Word (1925-1926)[40]

Background. After a brief stint at Göttingen, Barth received official notification from Berlin in mid-1925 that he been appointed as Professor of Dogmatics and New Testament Exegesis at Münster, Germany. Unlike his honorary position at Göttingen, Barth now had the status of being a full professor, with all rights and responsibilities, a post he maintained until 1930. It was during

---

[39]*CD* I/1, xiii.

[40]Karl Barth, *Witness to the Word: A Commentary on John 1* (Eugene, OR: Wipf & Stock, 2003). Originally published as Karl Barth, *Witness to the Word: A Commentary on John 1* (Grand Rapids: Eerdmans, 1986).

this time that Barth finished his dogmatic work begun at Göttingen, after which he turned his attention to lecturing in the history of dogmatics, dogmatics itself, and expositions of select New Testament books. Barth chose to lecture on the Gospel of John as soon as he arrived in Münster. Although he did not publish the lectures, they were posthumously edited and published in German in 1976, though only his commentary on the first chapter of the Gospel was translated into English in 1984. To be clear, Barth did not get past chapter eight in his lectures on the Gospel of John!

What to watch for. Those who have read both Barth's *Romans* and his lectures on John will note a marked difference in style, even in translation. Whereas reading *Romans* leaves one feeling assaulted by the utter contradiction of God and the gospel to human existence, Barth's John lectures read much more as one would expect of a professor of dogmatics and exegesis: detailed discussion of Greek grammar and philology, decisions on text criticism, references to Johannine scholarship, and careful exegetical/ theological argumentation. Consequently, *Witness to the Word* is far less literarily entertaining than *Romans*.

> Part of the servant form which is assumed is that the divine person who is flesh here takes it upon himself and is pleased to let himself be numbered self-evidently among the transgressors, to be seen as a companion of publicans and sinners, to be the reason for the most grievous offense. . . . His revelation cannot be known except with this danger of offense, since it can be known only in the flesh. Flesh would not be flesh without the full possibility of offense.
>
> *Witness to the Word*, 92-93, commenting on John 1:14

Nevertheless, Barth's theological moves in *Witness* are often breath-taking and theologically daring.

Although *Witness* demands much of its readers (and it is unfortunate that it has not yet received the scholarly attention it deserves), two important moves in Barth's exegesis are worth wrestling with. The first pertains to Barth's unique interpretation of John's use of the word *logos* ("Word") in the prologue, and the second pertains to Barth's insistence that there is no knowledge of Jesus Christ other than as the Word made flesh per se. You may at this point want to read the opening section before we turn to unpacking some of the major concepts found there.

The Logos as placeholder. The familiar opening of John's Gospel—"In the beginning was the Word, and the Word was with God, and the Word was God"—has potentially received greater attention in New Testament scholarship and interpretation than almost any other verse. In this regard, much scholarship has sought to identify what exactly John sought to denote through his use of the term *logos,* a word that had considerable religious and philosophical weight in his day. Did John seek intentionally to call those contemporary notions to mind for his readers and to apply them eventually to Jesus Christ? Barth is unconvinced by this line of argument. So, rather than seeking to peer into the deep meaning of *logos* as used in the cultural context of the first century and to discern the eternal nature of the *logos,* Barth instead seeks to deflect attention *away* from the question of *what* the *logos* is to the question of *how* John uses the term in his prologue.

Barth's answer, although far from achieving a scholarly consensus, introduces a fascinating alternative to the historic lines of interpretation: John introduces the concept of *logos,* with all its contemporary provocative philosophical and religious connotations, only shortly to dispense of it, never to return to it again in the Gospel. In other words, once the *logos* is identified as none other than Jesus of Nazareth, Barth argues, John no longer makes use of the concept in the remainder of the Gospel. According to Barth, John's use of the word *logos* serves as a quid pro quo ["this for that"]—a concept that temporarily stands in for another. As Barth puts it, "Already in the prologue *ho logos* is a substitute for Jesus Christ." Or as he says earlier, *logos* "is simply the provisional designation of a place which something or someone else will later fill."[41] The terminology of *logos*, he argues, is little more than a linguistic placeholder (*Platzhalter*) that John uses only until the identity of the one who is with God from the beginning, the one who is God (v. 1-2) and the one through whom all things are made (v. 3), is finally revealed as none other than the one made flesh, Jesus of Nazareth (v. 14, 17).

The logos *before Jesus?* The theological significance of Barth's move would be far reaching, yet probably even beyond his own immediate and full recognition. In essence, Barth demotes the terminology of *logos* from the heavy theological and linguistic burden scholarship has sought to make it bear. That is, Barth is suspicious of exegetical and critical attempts to identify what the *logos* meant to convey in the first-century context: "*What* was in the beginning, namely the Word and not something else, is not the point here. Instead, something is being said about the Word."[42] Consequently, Barth simply refuses to discuss the

> **EXPLORE FURTHER**
> For a recent discussion of Barth's perspective on the *logos*, see Darren O. Sumner, *Karl Barth and the Incarnation: Christology and the Humility of God*, 71-110.

---

[41]Ibid., 23.
[42]Barth, *Witness to the Word*, 19.

exegetical options that scholars have proposed about the meaning or identity of the Logos prior to the incarnation, as if the apostle were intending to give the reader insight into the nature of the pre-existent Christ. This is not, according to Barth, what John is intending to do.

Barth's reading of the function of John's use of *logos* as a temporary literary and linguistic placeholder pointing forward to the revelation of Jesus in the flesh is very probably the origin of what eventually has become a major point of contention among Barth interpreters: does Barth reject the concept of a pre-incarnate Logos as a theologically significant idea? Many in the history of the church's theology have divided Christology into its pre-incarnate and incarnate phases, with the pre-incarnate phase represented by the Logos, the second person of the Eternal Trinity, and the incarnate phase represented by the historical coming of Jesus of Nazareth. However, many of Barth's interpreters today now view the Barth of the *CD* as eventually coming to abandon the theological usefulness of a concept of a "pre-incarnate" or "fleshless Word" (*Logos asarkos*). Many others, however, argue that Barth continues to see the theological importance of a doctrine of the *Logos asarkos*, even if Barth finally prefers to speak more often of the centrality of the enfleshed Jesus Christ (*Logos ensarkos*) in our knowledge of God.

Although it is neither possible or desirable to unpack or adjudicate this technical

EXPLORE FURTHER
For one of the strongest defenses of Barth in favor of the *logos asarkos,* see Paul D. Molnar, *Divine Freedom and the Doctrine of the Immanent Trinity.* For the most important case in favor of the opposite position, see Bruce L. McCormack, "Grace and Being," in *The Cambridge Companion to Karl Barth.*

▶**Guretzki on the** *Logos Asarkos***:** My own perspective is that Barth, while writing the commentary on John's prologue, had not yet worked out the full implications of his exegesis for his Christology. Nevertheless, he was already beginning to sense its importance. Consequently, the evidence is ambiguous in *Witness* about whether Barth conceives of an "independent" *Logos asarkos* from the Incarnate Word, Jesus Christ of Nazareth. On the one hand, he says, "*Ho Logos* must remain the subject and the *sarx* the predicate. The Logos is what he is even without this predicate. The flesh exists in the concrete sense of the statement only as the predicate of the subject Logos" (90). The *Logos*, in other words, pre-exists the *Logos* enfleshed. On the other hand, Barth also insists, "Certainly we have to say that in every word that John writes he has in view Jesus of Nazareth as the reality that fills out his depiction of the function of the Logos, as the goal toward which he is moving. . . . John has been referring in a significant way to Jesus from the very first: *He* was in the beginning with God." (42). Thus, Barth also seems to indicate that there is no independent Logos apart from the man Jesus, who, in a way perhaps beyond our ability to comprehend, was with God from the beginning and not merely starting with his conception by the Holy Spirit in the womb of Mary.

debate here (though see the sidebar for my own conclusion), suffice it to say that readers who want to grapple with this concept in the *CD* will benefit from reading carefully Barth's arguments on the relation of the *logos asarkos* and the incarnate Jesus Christ first expressed here in Barth's lectures on John. Indeed, much of the exegesis in the John lectures eventually finds its way, often with little change, into the *CD*, especially in Barth's doctrine of election in *CD* II/2.[43]

Reading. Reading this text isn't particularly easy, but it is well worth the effort. Here I recommend reading pages 11-27, which includes a brief introduction and then Barth's unique reading of John 1:1 as we've discussed above.

The Holy Spirit and the Christian Life (1929)[44]

Background. Barth's move to Münster brought him into a new context of theological interlocutors. Whereas in Göttingen Barth was largely surrounded by Lutheran colleagues, in Münster he came into much closer contact with Roman Catholics, both informally through visitors he had in his home and formally with philosophers, theologians, and biblical scholars with whom he brushed shoulders daily at the university. By now, Barth had increasingly distanced himself from liberal Protestantism, especially in light of his concerted efforts to expound on and develop his own dogmatics. Barth's increased interest in and contact with Roman Catholic theology was also evidenced in at least two of his semesters of teaching. In the summer of 1926, he led a seminar on Anselm's *Cur Deus homo?* ("Why did God become human?") and in the winter of 1928–1929, his seminar was on Thomas

---

[43]Compare, for example, Barth's exegesis in *Witness* of John 1:1 (19-27) with his small-print section in *CD* II/2, 95-99.

[44]Karl Barth, *The Holy Spirit and the Christian Life* (Louisville, KY: Westminster John Knox Press, 1993).

Aquinas's magisterial *Summa Theologica*, a mainstay of Roman Catholic theology.[45]

Some months after Barth's Aquinas seminar, he delivered a lecture in October 1929 that was eventually published in English as *The Holy Spirit and the Christian Life: The Theological Basis of Ethics*. Hoyle, the translator, notes that the lecture sought to meet two criticisms that had been directed to Barth: that "Barth had no place for the Holy Spirit in his theology" and that "he had Catholic leanings."[46] This lecture, therefore, gives primary evidence of Barth's increased dialogue with Roman Catholics and, perhaps more importantly, demonstrates how Barth also sought to differentiate a Protestant doctrine of the Holy Spirit from what he saw in some of his contemporary Catholics. Most important in this regard is Barth's interaction with the Catholic philosopher-theologian Erich Przywara (pronounced, "Shah-VAIR-ah") who stood as a foil for certain elements of Catholic teaching that Barth sought to resist.

What to watch for. Barth's Holy Spirit–filled lecture is handily divided into three parts whereby Barth expounds on the Spirit as Creator, as Reconciler, and as Redeemer, which (surprise, surprise!) corresponds to the doctrine of God as Father, Son, and Holy Spirit. Readers will note that the themes of creation, reconciliation, and redemption also correlate to the major divisions of the third, fourth, and (projected but uncompleted) fifth volumes of his yet to be launched *CD*. So what are some important points to be observed in this little text?

First, in the section on the Spirit as Creator, Barth seeks to counter the idea that the image of God is something that permanently resides in the human being as part of her or his existence or as something permanently stamped deep on the human individual

---

[45]Bruce L. McCormack, *Karl Barth's Critically Realistic Dialectical Theology: Its Genesis and Development, 1909–1936* (Oxford: Clarendon Press, 1995), 378.
[46]Barth, *Holy Spirit*, xxi.

as a constituent part of who they are. Rather, the Holy Spirit is the one who is responsible to always freely give life to the human and to sustain the human as a creature. For Barth, this is the difference of making the Spirit into a permanent possession of humanity versus understanding the Spirit (as Barth would have it) as a promise, an ongoing occurrence of knowing oneself in relation to God by the gift of God's gracious revelation of himself to us. As Barth puts it,

> The sayings 'God has made us for himself' and 'man made in the image of God' are not to be taken as meaning an abiding and sure fact of revelation that we have once and for all made our own, but it is a process of revelation, which . . . is first coming to us and to come, moment by moment, if . . . we have taken seriously what is meant by the *Deity* of the *Creator* Spirit.[47]

It's evident in the first section that Barth calls into question Przywara's concept of the image of God as an *analogia entis* (analogy of being) between God and humans—a form of existence that humans share with God by virtue of being created in his image. However, it also stands as the formal beginnings of Barth's eventual primary reason for why he could not, finally, become a Roman Catholic. Indeed, by the time he begins his *CD* just a few short years later, Barth brazenly denounces the *analogia entis* as an "invention of the anti-christ."[48] To be sure, the emerging perspective of Barth in this text is also the basis on which he eventually distances himself from his friend Emil Brunner (to be discussed below), and it can be easy to assume that Barth has some of his own Protestant brethren in mind here. However, Barth's explicit referral to his Catholic colleague Przywara is evidence that Barth's primary target is what he understood as the Catholic doctrine of the *analogia entis*.

---

[47]Ibid., 5.
[48]*CD* I/1, xiii.

In section two, Barth argues that the Spirit of God is called *holy* not simply because of the Spirit's difference from creaturely existence but because the Spirit is in *"opposition* to the forceful and radical perversion and sin of the created spirit."[49] According to Barth, the Holy Spirit is the reconciler in his work because he alone is able to bridge the gap that exists between the Creator and the sinful creature. By definition, fallen humans are fallen precisely because they seek to make their own human action a "condition with regard to fellowship with God," and when this happens, "the Holy Spirit has been forgotten, [and] sin will be done to overcome sin."[50] Barth discerns this tendency to see oneself creating conditions for one's own reconciliation to God as the epitome of human religiosity—the hope that righteous works, even if not in totality, will bridge the gap, at least part way, between God and humanity. Barth identifies such attempts to combine divine and human action as stemming back to Pelagianism, but also, somewhat ironically, back to Augustine himself.[51] At any rate, Barth appears to discern that these same tendencies are at work in both Catholicism and Lutheranism, both of which by now he had become familiar with firsthand through his time at Göttingen and now at Münster. With this in mind, Barth warns,

> No psalm singing to the glory of God and no lowly knee
> bending can alter the fact that when God's grace and man's
> doing are looked upon as two sides of an affair, where one can
> turn it round and say, instead of the words "Holy Spirit," with

---

[49]Barth, *Holy Spirit*, 19.

[50]Ibid., 20.

[51]Pelagianism is "the teaching of British monk Pelagius (c. 354–415), who supposedly declared that human effort and merit could bring about salvation without divine grace." Stanley J. Grenz, David Guretzki, and Cherith Fee Nordling, "Pelagianism," in *Pocket Dictionary of Theological Terms* (Downers Grove, IL: InterVarsity Press, 1999), 89. The irony here is that Augustine was the one most famously known for his opposition to Pelagius.

just as good emphasis, "religious fervor," "moral earnestness," or even "man's creative activity"—then it is a simple fact that man has been handed over and left to his sins. You may cure a wound by such treatment but you cannot restore a dead man to life. And Augustine's view of sin was that it was really only a wound, a derangement within the undisturbed continuity of man with God.[52]

In contrast, Barth insists, the Holy Spirit is the "Finger of God" by which sinful humans, in their opposition to God's righteousness, are enabled to repent,[53] to believe,[54] and to obey.[55]

> **The Holy Spirit is absolutely and alone the umpire with reference to what is or is not the Christian life.**
>
> *The Holy Spirit and the Christian Life*, 37

Barth concludes in part three by pointing out that the Holy Spirit's holiness consists in no guise other than an *eschatological* one. That is to say, the Spirit as Redeemer is the Spirit of promise, the Spirit who alone can bridge the final barrier that stands between God and humanity—death. The Holy Spirit is the Redeemer because the Spirit will enact in the future what is only promised to us now in our baptism: the resurrection of the body to a future with God. It is because of this redeeming, eschatologically weighted work of the Spirit that Christians therefore have now been given three gifts as signs of the Spirit's eschatological presence: (1) the ability to respond to conscience, the anticipation of the future;[56]

---

[52]Ibid., 23.
[53]Ibid., 25-29.
[54]Ibid., 29-32.
[55]Ibid., 32-38.
[56]Ibid., 65.

(2) the ability to live in gratitude, the recognition that what we have is only ours by grace;[57] and (3) the ability to pray, to plead with the Father in light of his coming kingdom.[58]

In summary, Barth's lecture on the Holy Spirit brings together in one place several strands that had been emerging in the course of his early career. On the one hand, the lecture represents Barth's increasing resistance to any notion of a permanent point of contact or "givenness" between God and humans, and thus an increased resistance to what he perceived a key point of Roman Catholic theology: the analogy of being (*analogia entis*). On the other hand, Barth's Holy Spirit lecture provides solid evidence of the direction he was going to go in the construction of his *CD*. Although in the end the fifth volume—anticipated to be on the doctrine of the Holy Spirit as Redeemer—was never finished, this little lecture of Barth's provides us with at least some insights into where Barth would have gone had he lived long enough to carry out the project to its projected end. Those who want to examine Barth's pneumatology in the *CD* are encouraged to do so with this lecture also in hand.

Reading. The lecture alone—thirty-nine pages—of this extended three-part lecture should be easily read within an hour. Note that there are more footnotes to the lecture than most of Barth's writing, many of which contain interesting sidelights. However, these can be ignored if time is an issue. But promise me you will go back to them some day when you are able . . .

Anselm: Fides Quaerens Intellectum (1931)[59]

Background. In October 1929, Barth found himself once again in transition, this time with a move to the theological faculty at

---

[57]Ibid., 66.

[58]Ibid., 67.

[59]Karl Barth, *Anselm: Fides Quaerens Intellectum* (Pittsburgh, PA: The Pickwick Press, 1975).

Bonn, Germany. He remained at Bonn until the tumultuous mid-
1930s during the alarming rise of Hitler's National Socialist
movement. It had been during his tenure at Münster that Barth
attempted, a second time, to write a dogmatics, which he titled
Christian Dogmatics in Outline (*Die christliche Dogmatik im
Entwurf*).[60] However, shortly after his arrival at Bonn, Barth abandoned the project and, as he characteristically put it, "began again
at the beginning" when he finally started his *CD* in the early 1930s.

It was during this time that Barth completed this densely written
piece that he affectionately called his "little work on Anselm of
Canterbury."[61] The book paid particular attention to the so-called
proof for the existence of God as outlined in Anselm's book, *Proslogion*. Barth had lectured on Anselm's *Cur Deus homo?* in the
summer of 1926 at Münster, but he returned again to Anselm in the
summer of 1930.[62]

Scholars tracing Barth's theological development over the
course of his career have tended to see the book on Anselm as
marking a shift in his thought forms. This conclusion is supported both by Hans Urs von Balthasar's magisterial study of
Barth's development[63] and Barth's own affirmation of the importance of the Anselm book as "if not *the* key, then certainly *a* very
important key to understanding the movement of thought which
has urged itself upon me more and more in the *Church
Dogmatics*."[64] More recently, however, scholars have started to
view the Anselm book less as a shift in thought forms or concepts
for Barth and more as a clearer and more consistent outworking

---

[60]Not to be confused with his later work *Dogmatics in Outline* (New York: Harper Torchbooks, 1959). To date, *Die christliche Dogmatik im Entwurf* has not been translated
   into English.

[61]*CD* I/1, ix.

[62]McCormack, *Critically Realistic*, 415.

[63]Hans Urs von Balthasar, *The Theology of Karl Barth: Exposition and Interpretation*
   (San Francisco: Ignatius Press, 1992), 107.

[64]Barth, *Anselm*, 11.

of concepts and methods that had already been at work as far back as *Romans* or *The Göttingen Dogmatics*.[65] Our intention here is not to adjudicate this interpretive question of the significance of Barth's Anselm book as much as to highlight how the book itself seeks to correct what Barth saw as a wide Christian misreading of Anselm and his purposes. In other words, I encourage readers to engage Barth's commentary on Anselm especially to think through Barth's understanding of the significance and purpose (or function) of Anselm's so-called proofs of God's existence. In other words, read the book to better understand Anselm rather than Barth!

What to watch for. In his introduction, Barth sets the parameters of his inquiry on the proof of the existence of God in chapters two to four of *Proslogion*. For Barth, the main interpretive question to be answered is what "'to prove' means in Anselm generally."[66] In essence, Barth discerns that Anselm does not intend to provide an irrefutable "proof" (Latin, *probare, probatio*) of God's existence that any rational person could accept irrespective of her or his faith stance. On the contrary, Barth argues, Anselm is seeking to provide an account for *believers* by which they might gain a better understanding (*intelligere*) of the faith they already believe *(credo)*.

> Only in faith could [the] connection between the obedience of faith and the faith of the Church be experienced and only in experience could it be understood.
>
> **Anselm,** *Fides Quaerens Intellectum,* 35

The book itself is divided into two parts, plus a short introduction. In the first section, Barth seeks to provide his interpretation of Anselm's

---

[65]See especially McCormack, *Critically Realistic*, 421-49.
[66]Barth, *Anselm*, 14.

overall theological framework or "theological scheme." Barth discerns that Anselm has a particular understanding of the necessity, possibility, conditions, manner, and aims of theology. Most important for all this, Barth insists that Anselm sees the aim of theology as primarily and fundamentally giving explanation to the faith already believed and confessed in the church, not as an apologetic task of convincing those who do not, or refuse to, believe. Thus, Barth's interpretation of Anselm's theological stance is best summarized when he says,

> We will not find any passage in Anselm where he worked out the "proof," that is the argument directed outwards with the unbeliever in view, as an action that is different from the searchings that take faith itself as starting-point or where special "apologetic" action would follow on the "dogmatic." . . . The unbeliever's quest is not simply taken up in any casual fashion and incorporated into the theological task but all the way through it is in fact treated as identical with the question of the believer himself. . . . It was and remains quite impossible for Anselm to allow his faith to come to peaceable terms with lack of knowledge.[67]

In the second section of the work, Barth engages in an analytical commentary of the text of Anselm's proof as found in *Proslogion* 2–4. Readers should recall that Anselm's argument has been traditionally associated with the "ontological proof" of the existence of God, a form of argument that insists that the very concept of God itself—the greatest conceivable Being—must include with it the necessary attribute of existence. Anselm is not the only one to have argued in such directions, and later philosophers such as René Descartes and Gottfried Leibniz attempted similar forms of argument. However, unlike these later philosophers who indeed saw the argument as a

---

[67]Ibid., 67-68.

"rational proof," Barth refuses to see Anselm's argument in a similar light and, again, argues that Anselm's form of argumentation is on the basis of a presupposed, pre-existing belief in God's existence. Telling in this regard is Barth's observation that "Anselm thinks and proves in prayer and therefore not on logical presuppositions but by acceptance in practice of the existence of the One whose existence he undertakes to think out and prove."[68] In this vein, Barth discerns that what Anselm presupposed about the nature of theology is also that which Barth presupposes throughout the pages of his soon to emerge *CD:* God gives himself as an object of human knowledge, and God illumines humans so that they might know him as an object of knowledge. "Apart from this event there is no proof of the existence, that is of the reality of God."[69] So convinced is Barth of his interpretation that he ends the book by making a plea: stop putting Anselm's work in the same category as later philosophers like Descartes and Leibniz! While these theistic philosophers may in fact have sought to "prove" God's existence through recourse to rational argumentation, Anselm sought to better understand the faith he already had, and thus all such comparisons between Anselm and later philosophers of the ontological proof of God's existence are, Barth complains, "nonsense on which no more words ought to be wasted."[70]

Reading. It is my (deeply humble, of course) opinion as a longtime Barth reader that his book on Anselm is one of

EXPLORE FURTHER
For a helpful summary of the various forms of the ontological argument in history, see the *Stanford Encyclopedia of Philosophy* entry on "Ontological Arguments" at http://plato.stanford.edu/entries/ontological-arguments.

---

[68]Barth, *Anselm*, 101.
[69]Ibid., 171.
[70]Ibid.

his more difficult to read. It doesn't help that the text is littered with Latin citations (untranslated in the English translation) or that it is a very close and technical analysis of difficult theological concepts that require some background in medieval theology to comprehend. Nevertheless, it is identified by Barth as one of the texts that he "expended special care and devotion."[71] So, if it meant that much to him, we owe it to Barth to give it a try! For your assignment, tackle the opening pages (13-39) in the English edition.

"The Task of a History of Modern Protestant Theology" (1926, 1929)[72]

Background. In summer 1926, and then continuing to his last semester at Münster (winter 1929–1930), Barth gave a series of lectures on the history of Protestant theology since Schleiermacher.[73] The lectures themselves were eventually published in a complete collection in 1947,[74] but as Webster has noted, they remain a "strangely neglected text," even though it is the most extended work of historical theology that Barth ever published.[75] Indeed, the text of the newest English edition of the work runs 647 pages!

The full work is divided into two parts: "Background" and "History." In the first part, Barth outlines the background to the nineteenth century by examining selected thinkers from the eighteenth century, including Rousseau, Lessing, Kant, Herder, Novalis, and Hegel. When he commences on part two, Barth begins with the lengthiest of his chapters, the one on Schleiermacher, and beyond that eighteen additional nineteenth-century theologians,

---

[71]Ibid., 12.

[72]Karl Barth, "The Task of a History of Modern Protestant Theology," in *Protestant Theology in the Nineteenth Century*, trans. John Bowden, New Edition (London: SCM Press, 2001), 1-15.

[73]McCormack, *Critically Realistic*, 378.

[74]See Barth, *Protestant Theology.*

[75]John B. Webster, *Barth's Earlier Theology: Four Studies* (London; New York: T&T Clark, 2005), 93. See especially pp. 93-101 for Webster's analysis of the significance of Barth's *Protestant Theology in the Nineteenth Century.*

ending with Albrecht Ritschl. For our purposes, we will focus on Barth's opening essay, which can be read with great profit by theologians, pastors, church historians, and students of both theology and history alike.

What to watch for. In essence, Barth's essay outlines three claims, all made within the same paragraph.[76]

(1) *"There is no past in the Church, so there is no past in theology."* Barth's fundamental claim here must be understood as a theological claim, not a claim about the nature of time or history. Barth is not making an argument for the nonexistence of history (indeed, a difficult claim to support) but that, from the perspective of the doctrine of the communion of saints, all those who are in the church have a living voice, even if their body is dead and awaiting resurrection. In this regard the writings of Tertullian, Thomas Aquinas, Thomas à Kempis, Teresa of Ávila, Francis Turretin, and Ernst Troeltsch (including many others whose names do not start with "T") all speak in the present and are legitimate voices to be heard within the church. Although he does not state it as such, his claim is an implicit rejection of the idea of the "inevitable progress" of knowledge. That is, if one's voice today stands alongside the voice of those in the past, then we cannot stand in our time and place as a judge of the past voices nor presume that all that has been said before has either been wrong or has been leading up to the culmination of our present conclusions.[77]

(2) *"God is the Lord of the Church. He is also Lord of theology. We cannot anticipate which of our fellow-workers from the past are welcome in our own work and which are not."* Barth's plea here is

---

[76]Each of the three claims are taken from Barth, *Protestant Theology*, 3.

[77]C. S. Lewis once called this "chronological snobbery," which he defined as "the uncritical acceptance of the intellectual climate of our own age and the assumption that whatever has gone out of date is on that count discredited." C. S. Lewis, *Surprised by Joy: The Shape of My Early Life* (Houghton Mifflin Harcourt, 1966), 207.

simple but profound: as a theologian or historian, it is not our job to stand as judge and jury of past voices. Or, to put it positively, even if we have become convinced that we are in fundamental disagreement with certain Christian voices from the past and conclude that their theological position is in error, we cannot assume that we have nothing to learn from them as coparticipants in the Spirit's working in the church.

(3) *"For this reason, serious theological work is forced, again and again, to begin from the beginning."* This becomes Barth's rationale for why historical theology is such an important part of the theological task. It's not just to avoid the errors of the past but to ensure that we are taking our place as humble dialogue partners who not only speak our part but do our utmost also to listen, even to those whom we might at the outset presume to be wrong.

Did Barth live up to his own historical ideal? That is a question that will probably always be up for debate. But perhaps one of the most noteworthy examples of this was Barth's own lifelong critical yet respectful dialogue with the theologian Friedrich Schleiermacher. On the one hand, Barth insists in his essay on Schleiermacher that "it is impossible to consider Schleiermacher thoroughly without being strongly impressed. Indeed one is more strongly impressed every time one does consider him."[78] Yet within the same essay, Barth is nervous that in Schleiermacher's attempt to speak to the cultured despisers of religion of his day that he has finally capitulated to the demands of the culture rather than maintained his role as a theologian who is by definition supposed to be a proclaimer of the faith. Barth: "To put it metaphorically: as long as he is an apologist the theologian must renounce his theological function."[79]

---

[78]Barth, *Protestant Theology*, 412.
[79]Ibid., 428.

Perhaps what is most intriguing is that even in his last year of life, Barth was still engaging Schleiermacher. This is poignantly evident in a letter he wrote to his friend Carl Zuckmayer when he said, "Schleiermacher. . . . I am dealing with him in a seminar with many boy and girl students and for the moment I am enjoying it (with the old love/hate and the even older hate/love)."[80]

In the end, Barth was a fallen human like any other, and his disposition often led him to distance himself from even longtime friendships (such as with Emil Brunner, who will be dealt with shortly) over what he believed to be critical theological points of disagreement. Yet the fact of the matter is this: Barth engaged, and did not dismiss, even those with whom he felt he had to so sharply part company with.

Reading. When teaching courses on the history of theology in the past, I have assigned this entire essay for the first day of class. After completing the reading from Barth's "little book on Anselm," this one should be easy! Read the whole fifteen pages.

> **Neither the misguided theologian nor even the opponent of theology are excluded as incompetent—it is impossible to be an opponent of theology without being a theologian oneself—but only the idle onlooker who thinks that he can see and talk about something that does not concern him. . . . If his eyes are to be opened and he is to be entitled to join in the discussion, he must be involved in the matter.**
>
> "The Task of a History of Modern Protestant Theology," 2

---

[80]Karl Barth, *Karl Barth Letters 1961–1968* (Edinburgh; Grand Rapids: Eerdmans, 1981), 294.

"No!" (1934)[81]

Background. "No!" (*Nein!*) was actually written after the first half-volume of the *CD* (*CD* I/1) had already been completed and so is technically not a "pre-*CD*" work. I have included it here because of its widely acknowledged importance in the Karl Barth story and because it transitions nicely into the *CD* itself.

Emil Brunner was a friend and colleague whom Barth had known from his early years of pastoral work in Safenwil. Accord-

> There is between me and Barth no difference of opinion except the one on the side of Barth that there is a difference of opinion.
>
> **Emil Brunner,** *Natural Theology,* 18

ing to many theological observers, Barth and Brunner (along with Bultmann, Tillich, Gogarten, and others) represented together the new dialectical theology that was just beginning to be studied in the English-speaking world. However, by his own account, Barth perceived that Brunner was by 1929 "pursuing a theology that I increasingly came to view only as a return under a new banner to the fleshpots of the land of Egypt, which I thought that he had left behind once and for all in our common exodus."[82] This "other task of theology" that Barth assumed Brunner was returning to was what Brunner called "eristics" and what Barth called nothing more than a "heightened form of apologetics"[83]—or more seriously, an attempt to perceive the truth of God through the pursuit

---

[81]Karl Barth, "No!," in *Natural Theology: Comprising "Nature and Grace" by Professor Dr. Emil Brunner and the Reply "No!" By Dr. Karl Barth,* trans. Peter Fraenkel (Eugene, OR: Wipf & Stock Publishers, 2002), 65-128.

[82]As quoted in Busch, *Karl Barth,* 195.

[83]Ibid.

of "natural theology" rather than from God's own self-revelation in Jesus Christ.

The gap between Barth and Brunner continued to widen (at least in Barth's perception, if not Brunner's)[84] until 1934 when Barth wrote an angry response to Brunner's essay "Nature and Grace." Barth chose to title his response simply as "No! Answer to Emil Brunner," the implication of which was clear: Barth had drawn a line in the sand that he felt he could not cross. English readers are fortunate to have access to both essays together in one volume.

What to watch for. It's important to keep Brunner and Barth's essays closely connected: one can only properly understand Barth's piece by having first read Brunner's. Brunner seeks to lay out the issue (as he perceived it) that was emerging between him and Barth. In Brunner's estimation the dispute between them was about the extent to which the *imago Dei*—the image of God— remains in fallen humanity. Barth insisted that the image of God had been obliterated after sin, a point with which Brunner concurs.[85] However, Brunner goes on to argue that it is important to distinguish between the formal and material aspects of that image. Brunner argues that as a creature created in God's image, the human, even after the fall, continues *formally* (i.e., in appearance and form) to be a distinct and superior creature in the world, and as such, "has an immeasurable advantage over all creatures, even as a sinner, and this he has in common with God: he is a subject, a rational creature."[86] That said, Brunner continues to insist that from the perspective of the original justification that humans had with God is *materially* (i.e., really or actually) lost. "Materially the *imago* is completely lost, man is a

---

[84]Brunner and Barth, *Natural Theology*, 18.
[85]Ibid., 22-23.
[86]Ibid., 23.

sinner through and through and there is nothing in him which is not defiled by sin."[87]

From there, Brunner goes on to argue for what he sees as a Reformed version of *theologia naturalis* ("natural theology") "which tries to account for the phenomena of natural life" in humanity, even after the fall into sin.[88] For Brunner, it was a question of what way fallen humans can be addressed by their Creator God. Here he argues that though humans are materially and truly sinful, having lost their justification and righteousness before God, they are nevertheless human subjects capable of being spoken to by God and indeed, receiving God's Word to them. It is this form of the human's existence that Brunner sees as the *formal* image of God and that functions as a "point of contact" by which humans have "capacity for words and responsibility" before God.[89]

▶**Point of Contact:** The German term for "point of contact" is *Anknüpfungspunkt* [AWN-kennoop-foongs-poonked], which would be one of the sharpest points of dispute that Barth would eventually bring against Brunner. Though it was the Brunner-Barth debate that made the term notable, *Anknüpfungspunkt* and its English translation, "point of contact," had already been used extensively in both German and English literature on the theology of mission. See John G. Flett, *The Witness of God: The Trinity, Missio Dei, Karl Barth, and the Nature of Christian Community* (Grand Rapids: Eerdmans, 2010), 89-92.

---

[87]Ibid., 24.
[88]Ibid., 30.
[89]Ibid., 31.

It is difficult to know what Brunner expected from Barth, but almost certainly he did not expect the thunderous response he got. We cannot recount here in detail Barth's introduction to his response, but readers would do well to peruse it to get a sense from where Barth's anger was stemming. Although the matter may extend to deeper personal issues that possibly existed between Brunner and Barth, readers should note that Barth appears to be less angry with Brunner's argument per se—an argument that Barth clearly did not buy into—and more with having been pushed into a corner to respond. In my estimation, Barth's anger was probably a combination of his rejection of the possibilities of developing a "natural theology," which he felt was at root in what he saw as the "unhappy state of the Evangelical Church in Germany," and his displeasure in what he perceived as Brunner's tactic of appearing to be irenic in tone, including giving general praise to Barth while yet insisting that Barth had come to "false conclusions."[90] At any rate, there is evidence that Barth likely wanted to bypass answering Brunner's argument, which had been developing ever since at least 1929, but now felt that he was forced to respond, whether he wanted to or not.[91]

As you read Barth's response to Brunner, be aware that overall Barth sees three fundamental issues as problematic in Brunner's essay. The first is that Brunner ascribes a set of theses to Barth's

> I cannot agree with those who reproach Barth with ... "heresy-hunting." It is the result of his great devotion to his subject, and this not even his most embittered adversaries have been able to deny him.
>
> **Emil Brunner,** *Natural Theology,* 20

---

[90]Brunner and Barth, *Natural Theology,* 72.
[91]McCormack, *Critically Realistic,* 406.

position, which he admits Barth has never explicitly defended and which Barth refuses to recognize as properly representing his position. Barth is especially distraught that Brunner attributes to him a form of "natural theology" that Barth seeks explicitly now to deny: "Every attempt to assert a general revelation has to be rejected. . . . There is no point of contact for the redeeming action of God."[92]

This leads to Barth's second fundamental issue, which is theologically central, mainly, Brunner's notion of natural theology. Barth here substantially rejects the possibility that humans, even after the fall, have an inbuilt "capacity for revelation" or a "possibility of being addressed."[93] As we work our way through this portion of the essay, it should become clear that Barth's main point of contention is not merely a semantic dispute on what the words "capacity for revelation" (*Offenbarungsmächtigkeit* [O-fin-bar-oongs-maysh-teeg-kite]—say that ten times quickly!) or "point of contact" (*Anknüpfungspunkt*) mean, as important as this may be,[94] but rather to protect against the loss of the twin doctrines of *sola fide, sola gratia* ("by faith alone, by grace alone"), which insist that humans are justified before God— with nothing that they themselves contribute. As Barth insists, "If . . . there is an encounter and communion between God and man, then God himself must have created for it conditions which are not in the least supplied . . . by the

> ▶ ▶ ▶ **EXPLORER'S TIP**
>
> For a complete listing of the *Karl Barth-Gesamtausgabe* (i.e., the collected works of Karl Barth), see the Swiss publisher Theologischer Verlag Zürich at http://www.tvz -verlag.ch.

---

[92]Brunner and Barth, *Natural Theology*, 74.
[93]Ibid., 78.
[94]For a helpful attempt to unravel Brunner and Barth's perception of these central terms, see Trevor A. Hart, "A Capacity for Ambiguity: The Barth-Brunner Debate Revisited," *Tyndale Bulletin* 44, no. 2 (1993): 289-305.

existence of the formal factor [i.e., the formal image of God in humans that Brunner seeks to uphold]."[95]

The final issue that Barth deals with, though likely of secondary importance to the points just noted, is his dismay that Brunner appeals to the great Reformer John Calvin in favor of his own version of natural theology. Barth admits he is not a Calvin scholar and initially defers to an essay published by his brother Peter on the problem of natural theology in Calvin.[96] Nevertheless, Barth goes on to dispute Brunner's reading of Calvin on the basis that there is "an insufficient appreciation [by Brunner] of the place of the Reformers in the history of dogma"—a history, Barth argues, that needs to be understood in light of the Reformer's dispute with Roman Catholicism.[97] At any rate, Barth concludes his critique of Brunner's reading of Calvin by noting that Brunner has inappropriately brought Calvin to his side by a process that is "enough to make one weep"![98]

One footnote to this incident should be highlighted. Although it is likely Barth and Brunner's friendship was never the same afterwards, there does appear to have been steps taken toward healing of their relationship. I had the personal delight of sitting with Dr. John Hesselink (a former

> If I got rather lively, it was only because I really thought that there was some unity between Brunner and myself and that I could and should warn him against wantonly leaving the straight and narrow path. He may have been astonished at this, but I can tell him now that I then thought that he was still curable.
>
> *Natural Theology*, 71

---

[95]Brunner and Barth, *Natural Theology*, 89.
[96]Ibid., 100. The essay to which Barth defers is Peter Barth, "Allgemeine und besondere Offenbarung in Calvin's *Institutio*," *Evangelische Theologie*, 6 (1934): 189ff.
[97]Brunner and Barth, *Natural Theology*, 100.
[98]Ibid., 109.

student of both Barth and Brunner) who recounted the story of how years later, in 1960, he was able to both suggest and set up a reunion visit between Barth and Brunner at the Barth household. From every appearance, both Barth and Brunner, though initially apprehensive about the visit, were able to once again enjoy one another's company, including having a vigorous theological discussion![99]

Reading. If you can't read Barth's whole essay (which is just over sixty pages), then focus on the first twenty-eight pages (pp. 67-94). But I would rather you say no to reading only part of the essay and read the whole thing. Better yet, read Emil Brunner's essay first to get the whole picture.

Detour: Barth's Biblical Exegesis Outside the *Church Dogmatics*

Although we have limited this chapter to ten of Barth's pre-*CD* works, it's worth noting the extent to which Barth engaged in biblical exegesis. As we will see in the next chapter, Barth embeds a significant amount of exegesis in the *CD*. So I thought it would be helpful to take a short detour to consider how much exegesis he did even before he began his magnum opus. Let's take a look at Barth's biblical exegesis in his pre-*CD* sources.

Table 5.1 provides a compilation of Barth's exegetical works readily available in English, most of which are still in print as of the writing this book. Barth wrote various commentaries on either whole or parts of biblical books. Barth also produced lectures on other New Testament books that have, unfortunately, not yet been translated into English. These include lectures from James, 1 John, Colossians, 1 Peter, and the Sermon on the Mount. We can only hope that there will be dedicated translators in the near future who

---

[99]For a poignant retelling of the history of Barth and Brunner's relationship and reunion, see I. John Hesselink, "The Elephant and the Whale," *Reformed Journal* 12, no. 4 (April 1962): 4-7; and I. John Hesselink, "Karl Barth and Emil Brunner—a Tangled Tale with a Happy Ending (or, the Story of a Relationship)," in *How Karl Barth Changed My Mind,* ed. Donald K. McKim (Grand Rapids: Eerdmans, 1986), 131-142.

will take up the task of making these lectures available to English readers. Until then, you will either need to be able to read German or find someone who can do the translating for you.

Table 5.1. Karl Barth's biblical commentary material in English

Biblical Book or Passage	English Title	Originally Produced or Published (in German)	Notes
Luke 1	*The Great Promise: Luke 1*	1934, 1960	Originally a series of lectures given in 1934 but only published in 1960. English translation: 1963.
John 1	*Witness to the Word*	1925-1926	Originally a series of unpublished lectures on John 1-8, eventually published in 1976 and 1986. English translation (1986) only includes lectures on chapter 1.
Romans	*The Epistle to the Romans* (2nd through 6th editions)	1922	The first edition of Barth's Romans commentary (1919) is not translated into English. Second edition in English published in 1933.
Romans	*A Shorter Commentary on Romans*	1956	Barth's lesser-known *third* commentary on Romans based on lectures given in 1940-1941.
Romans 5	*Christ and Adam: Man and Humanity in Romans 5*	1952	Originally published as a longer journal article for *Theologische Studien*, and translated/published in English in 1956.
1 Corinthians 15	*The Resurrection of the Dead*	1924	Although focusing on 1 Corinthians 15, Barth has an extended introduction to the book on 1 Corinthians as a whole.
Ephesians	*Karl Barth's Academic Lectures on Ephesians Göttingen, 1921-1922*	1921-1922	An unpublished doctoral dissertation (2007) including a translation of Barth's lectures on Ephesians. Available at: http://hdl.handle.net/10023/399
Philippians	*Epistle to the Philippians*	1928	Lectures originally delivered in 1926-1927. English translation in 1947.

I mentioned earlier that when beginners to Barth delve into his commentaries, they quickly notice that his form of exegesis is noticeably different from the modern-day commentaries English readers are more accustomed to reading. Indeed, some of Barth's early critics wondered whether his commentary on Romans should even be designated as a commentary, so different was it from his contemporaries.[100] On the surface, Barth appears less interested in historical-critical matters, though to be clear he does emphasize that all these inquiries need to be taken seriously:

> In order to read and understand the Bible, biblical theology must conscientiously employ all known and available means, all the rules and criteria that are applicable to grammar, linguistics, and style, as well as all the knowledge gathered in the comparative study of the history of the world, of culture, and of literature.[101]

Barth's general (though not complete) silence on many of the detailed exegetical matters is not an indication of his ignorance of these matters, but in the end he was more concerned to press through to the substance of what the biblical authors were witnessing to as they wrote their texts. To put it another way, Barth tended to be less concerned with trying to discern what the biblical authors meant or what their original audience would have understood and more concerned with clarifying what aspect of God's self-revelation to which they were testifying or witnessing. In this regard, Barth's exegesis is generally not meant as an attempt to understand John, Paul, or James but an attempt to see and hear the very thing, or better, the very One, whom John, Paul, or James had seen and heard and to whom they were testifying. This is the reason that many have spoken of Barth's commentary as "theological exegesis" rather than "historical-exegesis" per se.[102]

---

[100]Burnett, *Barth's Exegesis*, 15.

[101]Barth, *Evangelical Theology*, 176.

[102]Here I point readers to the excellent study of Barth's so-called theological exegesis in his Romans period by Richard Burnett. Although it's a more advanced study, I have found no better explanation of Barth's hermeneutical methods and principles. See Burnett, *Barth's Exegesis*. However, see also Bruce L. McCormack, "The Significance of Karl Barth's Theological Exegesis of Philippians," in *Epistle to the Philippians* (Louisville: Westminster John Knox Press, 2002), v-xxv; and Francis Watson, "Barth's Philippians as Theological Exegesis," in *Epistle to the Philippians* (Louisville: Westminster John Knox Press, 2002), xxvi-li.

Given Barth's unique exegetical style, there are certain things you should and should not expect to get out of Barth. Let's start with a couple things you should *not* expect.

Barth is unlikely to delve into close examination of grammatical, syntactical, semantic, textual, or historical (i.e., critical) aspects the text. If you are interested in how a Greek word might have been used in extra-biblical material, whether a textual variant should or should not be accepted, or what the grammatical structure of a sentence might tell us about the verse's meaning, you will have to look elsewhere. That doesn't mean Barth ignored the Greek or Hebrew texts of Scriptures—he worked with the primary texts right from the beginning of his career. However, though Barth occasionally delves into these textual, linguistic, and literary matters that dominate historical-critical interpretation, these discussions are almost always either of secondary interest or meant only to set the stage for his more intensive attempt to interpret the theological significance of the text. That is, Barth is less concerned with the history of the text, or even the history underlying the text, and more concerned with what the text might have to say to readers *today.*

Barth is unlikely to give insight into the scholarly debates of his day. In some respects, this is not necessarily unique to Barth in his day. Academic convention, especially in North America in the last half-century, has dictated that biblical scholars demonstrate their awareness and expertise over issues in the field of biblical scholarship at large, usually manifest in detailed footnotes to other sources and lengthy discussions of scholarly debates. In this regard, Barth will on occasion make reference to other scholars when it supports his reading or when he feels he needs to make a particular point against a common consensus, but by and large, Barth will not give you depth of insight into what was happening in biblical scholarship in the early to middle parts of the twentieth

century. I suspect that this is not only because the scholarly con-
ventions were different but because Barth simply wasn't interested
in staking his place in theological academia. He is certainly not
afraid to dispute others, but neither does he go out of his way to
differentiate from or align himself with others unless he felt it was
absolutely necessary.

So what, then, can we expect?

**Barth has a tendency to make a major point, often repeatedly
and from a multitude of perspectives, throughout the commentary.** One of the best examples of this can be seen in Barth's
commentary on 1 Corinthians 15, published under the title of *The
Resurrection of the Dead.* There Barth devotes a good portion of the
book to make the argument that the entire book of 1 Corinthians
can only be understood properly as a lead up to chapter fifteen on
the resurrection, the "very peak and crown" of Paul's entire argument, mainly, that "the Resurrection of the Dead is the point
from which Paul is speaking and to which he points."[103]

Barth is usually more interested in the whole than the parts.
If there is a fault with some modern technical exegetical commentaries, it's that the author (and reader!) can often lose sight of the
theological forest in favor of the exegetical trees, and if there is a
fault with Barth, it's that he can sometimes be so attuned to the
theological forest that he fails to see the leaves of individual trees.
Of course, there are advantages and disadvantages to both ways of
doing a commentary, but as a reader of Barth, I have found that I
can more easily quibble with Barth on the details of his exegesis
than I can on his often breathtaking insights into the coherence of
the passage or book's message and the majestic way in which he
continually points us to Christ as he considers the biblical text.

---

[103]Karl Barth, *The Resurrection of the Dead* (Eugene, OR: Wipf & Stock Publishers,
2003), 101.

Barth always exegetes the text of Scripture with the assumption that it is the written Word of God to the church. Some of Barth's contemporaries (and some later as well) criticized Barth for largely ignoring the findings of historical critical scholarship on the Bible. Indeed, James Wharton once observed shortly after Barth's death that many biblical scholars who had become familiar with Barth's biblical expositions found his exegesis to be "offensive," if for no other reason than he so often went against the grain of his contemporaries.[104] Even his own son, Markus Barth, once remarked that his father's exegesis was often inconsistent and often contradictory.[105] Whatever problems this may pose (and it does pose some), it is probably best explained by virtue of Barth's expectation that Bible readers always need to go to the text of Scripture in anticipation of what fresh thing God might be saying today. In this regard, Barth was stubbornly committed to reading the Bible in order both to hear from God and to attempt to repeat to his contemporaries what he believed needed to be said from God today.

I finish this section with a quotation from Barth that beautifully illustrates what I think he was trying to do in his exegesis:

> We should not try to master the text. The Bible will become more and more mysterious to real exegetes. They will see all the depths and distances. They will constantly run up against the mystery before which *theology* is trying to drain the ocean with a spoon. The true exegete will face the text like an astonished child in a wonderful garden, not like an advocate of God who has seen all his files.[106]

---

[104]James A. Wharton, "Karl Barth as Exegete and His Influence on Biblical Interpretation," *Union Seminary Quarterly Review* 28, no. 1 (1972): 5.

[105]As cited by Warton. Ibid., 7.

[106]Karl Barth, *Homiletics* (Louisville, KY: Westminster John Knox Press, 1991), 128.

For Further Reading

Burnett, Richard E. *Karl Barth's Theological Exegesis*. Grand Rapids: Eerdmans, 2004.

McCormack, Bruce L. "Grace and Being: The Role of God's Gracious Election in Karl Barth's Theological Ontology." In *The Cambridge Companion to Karl Barth*, 92-110. Cambridge, UK: Cambridge University Press, 2000.

Migliore, Daniel I. "Karl Barth's First Lectures in Dogmatics: Instruction in the Christian Religion." In *The Göttingen Dogmatics: Instruction in the Christian Religion*, xv-lxii. Grand Rapids: Eerdmans, 1991.

Molnar, Paul D. *Divine Freedom and the Doctrine of the Immanent Trinity*. London and New York: T&T Clark, 2002.

Sumner, Darren O. *Karl Barth and the Incarnation: Christology and the Humility of God*. London and New York: Bloomsbury T&T Clark, 2014.

Webb, Stephen H. *Re-Figuring Theology: The Rhetoric of Karl Barth*. Albany: State University of New York Press, 1991.

Webster, John. "Karl Barth." In *Reading Romans Through the Centuries: From the Early Church to Karl Barth*, 205-23. Edited by Jeffrey P. Greenman and Timothy Larsen. Grand Rapids: Baker Books, 2005.

Part Two

Exploring the
CHURCH DOGMATICS

6

A Primer on Karl Barth's
Church Dogmatics

It's intimidating to see every volume of Karl Barth's *Church Dogmatics* huddled together on a shelf. I decided to do a quick measurement and found that the thirteen parts take up just under two feet of shelf space! In English translation, the text runs some 6,000,000 words and 8,353 pages (minus prefaces and indexes), so it is understandable why some give up reading even before they start. But I hope this chapter will give you the basic information you need to know about the *CD* as you get started.

Like any good travel guide, we begin by giving a broad overview of the topography of the *CD*, giving some attention to the structure and key features. After that, we'll delve into a few of the finer details and then finish the chapter with some suggested strategies for making the best gains without necessarily having to commit a decade to doing it.

Some Topographical Features of the *Church Dogmatics*

Let's start by understanding some of the more important topographical features of the landscape of the *CD*. First, unless you are proficient in Barth's native Swiss-German dialect, you are reading the *CD* in *translation*. That already presents some challenge, because no one person was assigned to translate the entire work into English. In fact, in the over three decades during which Barth was writing the *CD*, no less than seventeen individuals were involved in the English translation. That means some unevenness in translation can be observed, especially in the earlier volumes. However, we can be assured of two things: (1) the entire English translation was overseen by two individuals, Geoffrey Bromiley and T. F. Torrance, in whom Barth had significant trust; and (2) the entire fourth volume, in five parts, was translated by Bromiley himself, making it arguably the most reliably and consistently translated portion of the entire *CD*. You should also note that the very first volume, *CD* I/1, was subject to translation corrections and smoothing, such that a second edition of that early volume is now included in the set.

Second, it's helpful to know that the great bulk of the *CD* started as the content of lectures that Barth presented to his students over the decades. Indeed, knowing this helps to explain, at least in part, its nearly unfathomable length. In other words, the *CD* is like a transcript of an ongoing lecture some thirty-five years in length. (If you lectured every day for eight or ten months a year for thirty-five years, the transcript would be pretty long, too!) Knowing that the *CD* began as oral lectures can help readers catch some of its repetitions, reiterations, and other rhetorical routines. Remember also that Barth's audience would have been constantly changing over the

EXPLORE FURTHER

The final published text of the *Church Dogmatics (Kirchliche Dogmatik)* in German is 9,185 pages. According to Busch, it's nine times longer than Calvin's *Institutes of the Christian Religion* and almost twice as long as Thomas Aquinas's *Summa Theologica*.

years, so it shouldn't come as a surprise to us that he would have needed to repeat a few things here and there to get his audience caught up.

Third, because the bulk of the *CD* began as lectures, it's helpful to understand that Barth would begin each new section or "paragraph" (denoted in the English translations with the symbol §) with a carefully crafted series of sentences that functioned as a compact condensation of all that was to follow. Each opening sentence (or *Leitsatz*, literally, "basic principle") was meant to function as a thesis statement that students would dutifully copy verbatim and that could be referred back to throughout the course of the lecture as a reminder of what were the most important principles being discussed.

Fourth, reading the *CD* is greatly aided when one gets a handle on the structure of the whole work by paying attention to its outline. Although it took decades to write, Barth already had a firm sense of what the completed *CD* was going to look like, even if the details were far from being worked out. Fundamentally, the *CD*, as Barth intended it, was to be carried out in five volumes. (Keep in mind that "volumes" when referring to the *CD* doesn't refer to each individual book but to each major "topic." Thus, volume I was released in 2 parts, volume II in 2 parts, volume III in 4 parts, and volume IV in 4 parts!) The structure represented by the five volumes was as follows:

▸ ▸ ▸ **EXPLORER'S TIP**

Readers can access all seventy-three summary sentences (*Leitsatzen*) of the entire *CD* in the opening pages (1-13) of the index volume. It is recommended that beginning readers take time to read carefully and slowly through these paragraphs. Within a short time, you will already begin to have a flavor for the entire structure of the *CD*.

Volume I: *The Doctrine of the Word of God* (in parts 1 and 2)

Volume II: *The Doctrine of God* (in parts 1 and 2)

Volume III: *The Doctrine of Creation* (in parts 1, 2, 3, and 4)

Volume IV: *The Doctrine of Reconciliation* (in parts 1, 2, 3.1, 3.2, and 4; not finished)

[Volume V: *The Doctrine of Redemption* (never started)]

Two more notes on the *CD* as they are available to us in the English translation. First, Barth never finished the fourth volume on the doctrine of reconciliation. Technically, it is *CD* IV/3.2 that is the last link of a long unbroken chain of writing, even though another two books, *CD* IV/4 and the so-called *Lecture Fragments* of IV/4 exist. To be clear, *CD* IV/4 is technically a fragment and is devoted entirely to Barth's doctrine of baptism, but it was not actually the next logical section Barth intended to write. Therefore, the paragraph numbering (§) does not continue into IV/4, even though the "baptism fragment" itself is included in sets of the *CD* in English and German.

Second, although not included with the typical *CD* set, we are fortunate to have an English translation of the last paragraph in continuity with the *CD*. This section, "§74, The Command of God the Reconciler," published by Eerdmans under the title *The Christian Life*, includes lecture fragments in which Barth focuses his attention on an exposition of the meaning of the Lord's Prayer.[1]

▸ ▸ ▸ **EXPLORER'S TIP**

Those who use the *CD* a lot (scholars, pastors, students, etc.) usually cite the various parts using a shorthand system. Thus, *CD* IV/3.2 (or variations like *CD* IV.3/2 or *CD* 4.3.2) refers to the *CD*, fourth volume, third part, second half-part. This is the convention we are using throughout this guide.

---

[1] Karl Barth, *The Christian Life* (Grand Rapids: Eerdmans, 1981).

Structure of the *Church Dogmatics*

Although not necessarily immediately evident from the titles, the structure of the *CD* is implicitly trinitarian. While I will provide a brief summary of each volume in the "Guided Tour of the *Church Dogmatics*" in chapter eight below, some structural observations may help here. In volume I, *The Doctrine of the Word of God*, Barth sets up his entire project by arguing that "God reveals himself by himself" and that therefore any understanding of God will necessarily align with who God is as Father, Son, and Holy Spirit. Likewise, in volume II, *The Doctrine of God*, Barth argues that God's "being" and his "action" (i.e., who God is and what God does) can only be understood from who he reveals himself to be—Father, Son, and Holy Spirit. In volume III, Barth speaks about God the creator. God is none other than "God the Father, the Lord of his Creature." In volume IV, *The Doctrine of Reconciliation*, God is none other than Jesus Christ: servant, lord, and witness. Though he never began volume V, *The Doctrine of Redemption*, we do know that Barth intended to focus his work there on God the Holy Spirit.

Beyond this broadly trinitarian shape, it's also possible to discern a trinitarian pattern in each major volume. Although not 100 percent consistent, Barth starts each volume with a discussion of God's (i.e., the Father's) work (especially volumes II, III, and IV), carries on with a discussion of Jesus Christ, and ends with a discussion of ethics, often implicitly or explicitly connected to the work of the Holy Spirit. Barth was, in other words, fairly consistently concerned not only

EXPLORE FURTHER
The *CD* was also being translated into French and Japanese even as Barth continued to churn out volumes in the mid-1950s to mid-1960s.

that his dogmatics be molded by the shape of God's own triune self-revelation but that dogmatics also be an exercise in asking what God demands, or commands, of the listening human to God's Spirit. Thus, volume I ends with a discussion of the proclamation of the church while volumes II, III, and IV each end with a discussion of the commandment of God, the commandment of the Creator, and the commandment of the Reconciler. One can safely presume, had Barth completed volume V on redemption, he would have finished it with a discussion of the commandment of God the Redeemer.

Finally, and in some respects, most importantly, beginning readers need to become keenly attuned to the fact that Barth wrote a *church* dogmatics. That is to say, Barth understood the role of the theologian to be a servant to the mission of the church. Theology was not, as some in the universities of his day (or today!) might assume, an independent discipline that answered only to those within the guild of theologians. On the contrary, theology—dogmatics—was undertaken in service to the church.[2] As I have noted elsewhere, Barth insisted that a theology that did not aid the preacher or teacher in proclaiming the gospel was a theology that had already lost its moorings.[3] Or as Barth once explained, "No single item of Christian doctrine is legitimately grounded, or rightly developed or expounded, unless it

> Barth understood the role of the theologian to be a servant to the mission of the church.

---

[2] See **dogmatics** in chapter 4 above.
[3] David Guretzki, "Become Conversant with Barth's Church Dogmatics: A Primer," in *Karl Barth in Conversation*, ed. W. Travis McMaken and David W. Congdon (Eugene, OR: Wipf & Stock, 2014), 287.

can of itself be understood and explained as part of the responsibility laid upon the hearing and teaching Church towards the self-revelation of God attested in Holy Scripture."[4]

Some Finer Features of the *Church Dogmatics*

With these fundamental features of the *CD* in mind, it is also helpful to become acquainted with some of its more technical features, some of which might seem foreign to twenty-first-century readers.

The significance of . . . font sizes. Anyone who has done any level of academic work in theology or the humanities knows how important documenting one's sources are. Most modern scholars cite their sources in carefully formatted footnotes or endnotes. However, you will look in vain for such notes in Barth's *CD*. This doesn't mean that Barth simply ignored other theologians or scholars but that it was acceptable in his day and age to cite authors as needed without necessarily giving extensive bibliographic information. (Barth would likely never get away with doing such things today!)

What Barth does do, however, is something that new readers of the *CD* quickly notice: he separates the text into two distinct font sizes. Scholars and longtime Barth readers have very clever names for these sections: "small print" and "large print" sections! So what is the purpose of these two differing font sizes?

Simply put, the large-print sections represent the main flow of Barth's theological argument while the small-print sections tend to reveal more of the "technical" details—details such as historical references to other theologians, major points of theological dispute in recent or earlier church history, or detailed exegesis of scriptural passages. Barth is rumored to once have said that people who don't have time to read the entire *CD* could benefit by reading

---

[4]*CD* II/2, 35.

just the large print sections. But let me suggest that you *not* take Barth's advice! In my experience, I can attest that some of the most moving and earth-shattering observations come from those small-print sections.

Greek, Hebrew, Latin, etc. If you have one of the standard copies of the *CD*, you will quickly have to come to grips with the reality that Barth was fond of citing biblical texts in Greek or Hebrew. Other times Barth will cite important ancient, medieval, or Reformed sources in Latin, usually in the small-print sections. (For a sample of how far Barth will sometimes go in citing the Latin, take a look at the small-print section on pages 60-70 of *CD* II/1, where not a single page is without some Latin citation. Some pages—e.g., p. 63—contain almost more Latin text than English.)

Clearly, if you are unable to read the biblical languages or ecclesiastical Latin, this poses some challenge. Fortunately, apart from learning the languages yourself (which isn't a bad idea, but I understand that not everyone has the time!), it is possible to read through the *CD* without having to understand the foreign language sections, especially since most of the citations tend to be support given by Barth for a particular point, and then usually in the small-print sections. You may occasionally miss a finer point he is trying to make, but you can probably also pick up the gist of what he is saying in context. For those readers who can remember the good ol' days, being able to read the Greek and Latin is a bit like the difference between watching color and black-and-white TV: You get the picture in both instances, but one is just prettier!

> ▸ ▸ ▸ **EXPLORER'S TIP**
>
> Instead of skipping the Greek and Latin, I recommend gaining access to a digital edition of the *CD*. See "Other Karl Barth Resources" in chapter nine below.

It's also the case that the longer Barth wrote, the less he tended to include those long foreign citations. So by the time you get to volume IV on the doctrine of reconciliation, Latin and Greek texts are far less common.

Use the index! I am somewhat embarrassed to tell you that it was quite some time into my study of Barth's *CD* before I discovered the usefulness of the index volume (the fourteenth part) that accompanies the *CD*. It's not that I didn't know it existed, it's just that I assumed it was only a compilation of all the indexes already at the end of each volume. The fact is, the index volume was recompiled and expanded upon completion of the full translation. Consequently, while the indexes at the end of each volume are helpful to a point, you should be sure to consult the more complete index volume whenever you can. I will also mention in chapter seven below that there are many more treasures and features found in the index volume. The moral of the story is simple: use the index!

> ▸ ▸ ▸ **EXPLORER'S TIP**
>
> If you can gain access to an electronic format (such as from logos.com or alexanderstreet.com), you will not only have access to Latin and Greek translations but can do custom Boolean and context searches above and beyond the limitations of the printed index.

Starting to Read the *Church Dogmatics*: Some Hints

I've been asked many times the best way to start reading Barth's *CD*. Because the work is so massive, there's a danger that those starting from page one of volume I will find themselves a bit discouraged when, after nearly three hundred pages, they still haven't yet gotten to the doctrine of the Trinity. It is a little like trying to read the Bible for the very first time, starting at Genesis, and getting bogged down somewhere in a genealogy in Numbers. So is there a better way to do it?

Although Barth would have probably preferred we read the *CD* in the order written, beginners in Barth shouldn't feel like they need to read it from beginning to end. Indeed, one of the best ways to get into reading Barth is to select a section that may be of interest and begin there.

Most longtime readers of Barth have a favorite section or volume, but where do you begin if you have no experience? In the opening pages of the index volume we have all of the headings and thesis statements (*Leitsatz*) readily provided. Thus, for example, if you are interested in what Barth might have said about angels, you might want to check out §51 (in *CD* III/3), "The Kingdom of Heaven, God's Messengers and Their Adversaries." Or maybe you are interested in what Barth has to say about the Holy Spirit. In that case, start with §12, "God the Holy Spirit," found in *CD* I/1. Whatever your interest, perusing this part of the index is a good way to get acquainted very quickly with the overall content of the *CD*.

I also suggest, cautiously, that beginning readers take advantage of Geoffrey Bromiley's now classic work, *Introduction to the Theology of Karl Barth*. Bromiley's text is unlike any other book on Barth inasmuch as Bromiley seeks to do little else than to provide short synopses, section by section, of the entire *CD*. Bromiley only occasionally adds editorial comments or questions and seeks rather to stick to simple summaries. Such summaries can be extremely helpful to the reader who is feeling overwhelmed before she even starts. Spending a few minutes reading through the appropriate section in Bromiley's work can function somewhat like another good travel guide: it gives you at least a basic sense of what to expect and to make sense of what you are reading as you move along. However, as I mentioned above, I recommend that Bromiley be used with caution. This isn't because Bromiley is not to be trusted;

on the contrary, he was keenly acquainted with the *CD* as perhaps no other person ever was because of his longtime friendship with Barth and as one of the primary English translators and editors. However, Bromiley is *not* a replacement for Barth. Do not assume, in other words, that just because you have read Bromiley's summary that you "get" Barth any more than reading a traveler's guidebook is a replacement for actually seeing the sights.

Once you have gotten a taste of Barth from two or three sections, it is probably time to commit to reading a full volume or at least a part volume from beginning to end. Although advice will vary depending on who you talk to, there are certain sections that are widely acknowledged to be among Barth's best. However, let me suggest three sections to read that will give you significant mileage in understanding Barth's theological project as a whole.

The Revelation of God *(CD I/1, §§8-12).* In this early section of the *CD*, Barth makes a threefold axiomatic statement—namely, (1) that God is known by how he reveals himself; (2) that God reveals himself by himself; and (3) that God reveals himself as the Lord, the Lord who is Father, Son, and Holy Spirit. That God reveals himself as Lord is what Barth calls "the root of the doctrine of the Trinity." This section is important in understanding how Barth sees revelation itself as trinitarian in shape and tied to God's own action. Revelation is not something outside of God but is something that God himself does by himself and for our sake.

God's Gracious Election *(CD II/2, §§32-35).* As important as Barth's doctrine of triune revelation is, a good number of scholars today argue that Barth's doctrine of election may well go down in history as his most significant contribution to the history of theology. Although still debated, some even go so far as to argue that in his doctrine of election we see a significant shift in Barth's theology—a shift that affected the outworking of the rest of the *CD*. Whatever future historians of doctrine might say, Barth's breathtaking doctrine of election should not to be missed. Indeed, I would argue that if you can read only one section of the *CD*, it should be this one.

Why is Barth's doctrine of election so important? Suffice it here to recognize that Barth insists that not only is Jesus Christ the *object* of God's gracious election, the one God chooses to carry out his purposes in salvation (something that theologians have long recognized), but Barth also insists that Jesus Christ is to be reckoned as the *subject* of election, the one who is doing the electing. Beyond this important identification of Jesus Christ as both the Elected Man and the Electing God, Barth also emphasizes that election must be understood first as concerning Jesus Christ, second the community, and only third the individual. While earlier Reformed doctrines of election tended to focus on the doctrine of double predestination—a doctrine of election that suggests that some individuals are elect to be saved and others are elect to be damned—Barth seeks to introduce a correction to the Reformed doctrine of election. It's not that Barth rejects double predestination but that he applies both election and rejection first and foremost to Jesus Christ—the one who is both elected and rejected for our sake, and in whom all, secondarily, are elect. Whether in the end you agree or disagree with Barth, the doctrine of election hereafter cannot/should not be discussed without reference to Barth.

**The Doctrine of Reconciliation *(CD* IV/1, §§57-63*).* Although Barth's doctrine of election is widely acknowledged to be the most theologically groundbreaking, it's in his doctrine of reconciliation, particularly the first part of volume IV, that we reach the majestic and beautiful heights of Barth's theology. Even before he launches into the doctrine with full energy, Barth attempts a survey of the whole doctrine in §58. Reading this section alone will orient readers to the subject matter that Barth devoted the rest of his life to working out.

Once §58 is completed, readers are taken on a breathtaking journey with Jesus Christ into the "far country." Here Barth alludes to the parable of the prodigal son (which interestingly he does not fully acknowledge until *CD* IV/2 §64 in a section titled "The Homecoming of the Son of Man") and gives the parable a christological reading. Barth's ingenious way of looking at the parable is to note that though the son in the parable is the prodigal, his movement parallels that of Jesus' own movement: going out from the Father to the far country of this world, only to return to the Father having completed his mission and being exalted in his return.

7

A User's Guide
to the *Church Dogmatics*

Saint Augustine once made the claim that some things are meant to be enjoyed and some things are meant to be used. The problem is, he said, sometimes we enjoy the things that are supposed to be used, and use the things that are supposed to be enjoyed. In both instances our "course will be impeded and sometimes deflected."[1]

With this Augustinian distinction in mind, I would like to make a simple claim: *Karl Barth's* Church Dogmatics, *even if enjoyed, is finally meant to be used.* (I will admit that reading Barth isn't *always* an enjoyable experience, but his work is almost always of great use to me.)

That might seem like an odd kind of claim to make. Are not theological treatises meant to be *read?* Indeed, any *use* of the *CD* means taking the preliminary step of *reading*

> Merciful God, I ask that thou wilt grant me, as thou pleases, to seek earnestly, to investigate carefully, to know truthfully, and to present perfectly, to the glory of thy name, amen.
>
> **Thomas Aquinas**

---

[1]Augustine, *On Christian Doctrine* (Upper Saddle River, NJ: Prentice-Hall, 1958), 9.

it, but Barth himself was insistent that theology, for it to be a truly *good* theology, needed to present itself humbly in service to the church and her mission. Good theology, in other words, is not to be upheld as an end unto itself, no matter how beautiful or profound or intellectually ground-shaking it is perceived to be. Consequently, we honor Barth's work when we read it as he hoped it would be read: as an aid or instrument to a greater ecclesiological end, whether that end is the preparation of a sermon in which the gospel is proclaimed; the teaching of a college or seminary class in which the truth of Christ is explored; the explanation of a theological concept to a confirmation, youth, or children's class; the writing of a hymn or spiritual song meant to edify and encourage God's people; or the comforting of a soul in need of pastoral care and a spoken Word (word) from God. That means that as much as we might admire the Swiss theologian for his depth, beauty, and insight (or conversely, chastise him for his opaqueness, length, or inconsistency), in the end the *CD* is read aright when used as a theological tool, not necessarily as an artifact to be viewed in and of itself.

With the foregoing in mind, this chapter seeks to guide readers into responsible use of the *CD* in two important churchly activities: in biblical exegesis and in preaching. We will then consider the value of a Barth reading group, followed by some guidance on doing theological papers on the *CD* in an educational context.

The *Church Dogmatics* and Biblical Exegesis

In his provocative lectures in America in 1962 (and subsequently transcribed and expanded in *Evangelical Theology: An Introduction*), Barth describes the work of doing biblical exegesis as "the fundamental task of all theological study."[2] Barth, of course, is most widely

---

[2]Karl Barth, *Evangelical Theology: An Introduction* (New York: Holt, Rinehart and Winston, 1963), 175.

known as a theologian, but those beginning to read Karl Barth may
not realize three important points. First, Barth spent the early
portion of his career as a pastor who was called on week in and week
out to produce sermons. He began his theological pilgrimage, in
other words, in the pulpit rather than the podium. Second, Barth
wrote a significant amount of biblical commentary. Beyond his
well-known commentary on Romans, he also wrote commentaries
on Philippians, 1 Corinthians 15, and the first eight chapters of the
Gospel of John, and he wrote numerous unpublished lectures presented on various New Testament books.[3] Third, and more to the
point, the CD is filled with biblical exegesis. Indeed, the Scripture
index volume of the CD stretches over 170 pages alone and includes
some 15,000 biblical references (keeping in mind there are approximately 31,000 verses in the entire Bible). In addition, although
there are many verses and passages dealt with only once, many passages are dealt with numerous times over the course of the CD.

So how can Barth be responsibly used in exegesis of a biblical
passage, whether in sermon or lesson preparation or in academic
exegetical papers?

Exegesis in the *Church Dogmatics*

There is much exegesis embedded in the CD, but it's important to
understand that it's somewhat different from his commentary and
lectures on biblical books. Here the index volume to the CD is the
exegete's best companion! There scriptural texts are listed in ca-
nonical order, with references to places in the CD where Barth has
either directly dealt with or provided exegesis of the passage or
indirectly made allusions to the text. The format of the index is
such that allusions to whole chapters or even multiple chapters are
dealt with first, and then individual verses dealt with next. Beyond

---

[3]For more about Barth's exegesis, see "Detour: Barth's Biblical Exegesis Outside the CD"
in chapter 5 above.

this, each entry is followed by a first column in which the print is usually in bold, designating locations in the *CD* where the text is dealt with directly as a significant exposition of that text. This is followed by a second column to the right listing additional secondary references to the text, most of which are simply citations or allusions to the text. Finally, in that column, some entries are marked with an asterisk, which means that the section being indexed may not directly mention the verse, but it discusses a matter that the editors have judged to be pertinent to the understanding of that text.

An excerpt drawn from an entry on the first page of the Scripture reference index (Genesis) will illustrate how best to use the index. See table 7.1.

Table 7.1. Scripture reference index

Chapters	Primary Exposition	Secondary Expositions or Allusions
1–2	**II,1: 104**	II,1:117; III,1:20f., 63, 84-87*, 103, 229; III,2:8f.*, 14, 446,458; III,4: 159*, 310f., IV,2:588
1–11	**IV,3: 688f.**	III,4:312, 317
1³* * i.e., Chapter 1:3	**III,3: 73f., 382**	I,1:42 (45); III,1:33, 152 f., 161; III,3: 382; IV,1: 306; IV,3:145

We see, for example, that chapters 1–11 of Genesis are dealt with as a whole or as a section in an extended treatment in volume IV part 3 on pages 688 and following (=f.). Secondary treatment or mention of Genesis 1–11 as a whole is mentioned on pages 312 and 317 of volume III/4. However, if we wanted to check out Barth's treatment of Genesis 1:3, we would head over to volume III/3, especially on pages 73 and 382. If we had time, we could also check out the multiple secondary references in five other part-volumes noted to the far right.

Preaching and the *Church Dogmatics*

As already noted, Karl Barth was convinced that the task of dogmatics was meant to serve the church's broader task of proclaiming the gospel. Dogmatics was for Barth a kind of "second order" language subservient to the "first order" language of church proclamation. That said, Barth did produce a little book on homiletics, the art of sermon preparation, though frankly, in my opinion and in the opinion of many professional homileticians, it wasn't his best work.[4]

Nevertheless, with Barth's distinction between preaching and dogmatics in mind, it is worth observing his own practice of preaching by reading through some of his more mature sermons, which are available in different sources.[5] It should be clear very quickly that Barth's sermons are stylistically quite unlike his actual dogmatics. That is because Barth was of the mindset that dogmatics seeks to examine the content of church preaching against the canon of Scripture but that preaching does not somehow need to conform to the canons of dogmatics. A sermon, in other words, is neither a lecture nor a recounting of exegesis but a declaration—a proclamation—

> **EXPLORE FURTHER**
>
> For an extensive and generally positive consideration of Barth on preaching, see William H. Willimon, *Conversations with Barth on Preaching*.

---

[4]Karl Barth, *Homiletics* (Louisville, KY: Westminster John Knox Press, 1991).

[5]Three such sources of sermons include William H. Willimon and Karl Barth, *The Early Preaching of Karl Barth: Fourteen Sermons with Commentary by William H. Willimon*, trans. John Elbert Wilson (Louisville, KY: Westminster John Knox Press, 2009); Karl Barth, *Deliverance to the Captives* (Hymns Ancient & Modern Limited, 2012); and Karl Barth, *Call for God: New Sermons from Basel Prison* (Hymns Ancient & Modern Limited, 2012). The latter two of these are sermons that Barth preached to prisoners in Basel.

of what the preacher sought to hear God saying in and through Scripture for her or his hearers today. This is why Barth can say, "One cannot and should not expect to hear the content of proclamation from dogmatics."[6] In this regard, Barth gives some excellent advice to any and all preachers, whether beginners or veterans:

> It is a familiar and perhaps unavoidable beginner's mistake of students and assistants, when preaching, to think that they can and should confidently take the content of their preaching from their treasured college notebooks and textbooks of dogmatics. On the other hand, older preachers are usually far too confident in removing themselves from the jurisdiction of this critical authority.[7]

So where does this leave us in terms of how to use the *CD* in preparation of sermons? I offer two simple guidelines here.

Make use of the Scripture indexes and the Aids for the Preacher. In addition to the fantastic resource of the Scripture index, make sure you become familiar with the "Aids for the Preacher" found in the index volume. This resource, which is often overlooked by preachers, can be of some value, particularly for those who follow the liturgical year. It allows preachers to see if their text for the particular Sunday in the church calendar is included. If it is, the editors have included exegetical excerpts from the *CD* that may help illuminate the text. It takes only a minute to check each week, and if a text is discussed, great! You don't even have to dig out the other volumes. If not, you can move on to your other exegetical sources and commentaries.

Quotations from Barth's CD should be rare in a sermon. That advice may come as a surprise, coming as it is from someone who so appreciates his work. But the practical reality is, most

---

[6]*CD* I/1, 79.
[7]Ibid.

people (even if not all) in the pew really don't care what Karl Barth said. And Karl Barth himself probably would be embarrassed to know that he is sometimes quoted extensively. Instead, I recommend that Barth quotations be rare, and when he is cited, we should stick to one of his more memorable turns of phrase rather than trying to read a lengthy section that most hearers will likely be unable to digest.

Remember that responsible use of the CD is meant to help you clarify what is being preached against the Scriptures and the voices from the past, but it is not necessarily meant to be a source for filling out the sermon, nor for gaining intellectual kudos from the more academically oriented in your congregation. In short, the CD is best used from Monday to Saturday but should be safely stowed on Sunday morning!

Doing the *Church Dogmatics* Together:
Starting a Barth Reading Group

It has been my privilege and pleasure to lead a Karl Barth reading group for a decade straight, with no sign of finishing any time soon. The journey has been rich for me and, I hope, for many of the participants who have journeyed with me. In my context, I have had college and seminary students, fellow faculty, pastors, and other community members join in. I realize that not everyone lives in a context that makes running these groups as easy as I have had, living and working on a college and seminary campus as I have for over twenty years. Nevertheless, I commend starting and running a group as a great way to teach and learn from Barth together.

One of the reasons a Barth reading group can be so effective, especially if reading the CD together, is precisely because Barth originally wrote the CD as an ongoing series of oral lectures delivered in a classroom or lecture hall. And I can't prove it, but I believe we get more from the CD (and indeed, from any classic text) when we can slow down and take some time to discuss what Barth has written (especially over a preferred hot or cold beverage). Even more important, I think we need to learn to discuss the theological matters Barth is talking about for ourselves. As important as it is to "understand" what Barth said, it's even more important to figure out if what he has said is true or helpful to our own context and discipleship.

As for practical tips on how to run a group, let me suggest a few things that I have learned over the years.

- Given my context on a college and seminary campus, I've run my group to coincide with the academic year, roughly from September to April, and we've met weekly with appropriate breaks at Christmas, Easter, and so on. You needn't follow that schedule on your own, but I do believe that optimally, a weekly meeting is best. I started with the intention of meeting every two weeks, but that was too long of a gap in between meetings. Once we settled nicely into a weekly meeting, we never turned back.

- At the outset of each year, as a group, we select a volume to read together or carry on from an unfinished volume from the previous year. Then, week by week, we move through the volume with a pace of about five to ten pages of text. Again, at times I have tried to get through more each week, but there is usually plenty to discuss, and anything more than ten pages is likely too much to discuss in a short time. As for the length of our time together, I have generally tried to take seventy-five minutes, but of course, what you spend will depend on your own situation. My experience says that thirty minutes is too short, and ninety minutes is a bit too long, so probably anywhere between sixty and seventy-five minutes is probably about right.

- Meeting place is important, too, and the surroundings will definitely dictate the mood. If you want dead serious discussion, you might need a classroom in a church or school. If you want a bit more leisurely discussion, the coffee shop or pub works fine. Just know that the context will affect how the group functions and whether it is more or less formal.

- As for the pattern of meetings, ours has been quite simple. Early on in my Barth reading group, I created a set of three rules which we have followed unwaveringly ever since and of which I remind the group each year, especially since I usually have new members joining while others may need to drop out. The rules are:

(1) *We are all co-learners, but I retain the rights as leader of the group.* Rule 1 is simply meant to give a sense of the kind of environment I wish to create. The group has gathered to learn together, not to hear a lecture from the group leader. That means that equal preparation on the part of everyone is expected, and that also means that the best co-learning happens when everyone commits to reading the selected section ahead of time. As for the second part of rule 1, I've been fortunate to have rarely needed to invoke my "authority" as group leader, but it has on occasion happened when someone begins to dominate unhelpfully, or a friendly debate turns less than friendly. In such instances, I have tried to deal with the issue outside of the group, but thankfully, I haven't had to worry about this too much. I simply say, better to be prepared for the possibility of ugly conflict or of having someone dominate discussion to the detriment of others than to be unprepared to deal with it.

(2) *We commit, as much as possible, to attend regularly for the benefit of all participants.* Rule 2's purpose should be self-evident: because the Barth reading group is voluntary, it can sometimes be easy to skip when life gets a bit too busy or other priorities seem more urgent. But I make clear

at the outset of each year that we are committing to coming regularly, not just to make me feel good but because we are committing to one another's learning. In my experience, this has actually resulted in a high degree of commitment, recognizing that, life being what it is, not everyone can always make it to the meeting every week. However, setting out this expectation at the outset helps members to tend to their own schedules accordingly.

(3) *We begin each meeting with Scripture and prayer, and end each meeting with prayer.* I have set this third rule to honor what I believe was Barth's twofold view of the purpose of theology: to serve and build up the body of Christ and to enable us to be better readers of Scripture. In that regard, I have intentionally begun each meeting time with a selection from Scripture. For us, that has usually meant working sequentially through a book of the Bible throughout the year. Usually, I spend very little time, if at all, expositing the Scripture, though occasionally I will make comment or open the group up to comments. What has been interesting is how often the Scripture relates in serendipitous ways to something we are reading in the *CD* itself. Of course, one could follow a liturgical reading schedule or read a psalm each week, but whatever Scripture is chosen, it has been my goal to signal to participants that Scripture, not Barth, is the *norming norm* by which all theology is measured. Although I cannot confirm it, I happen to think Barth would have been happy to know that we did this.

- More importantly, I have sought to begin and end each session with prayer. Sometimes I have asked for prayer requests, other times I have not. I will often ask a group member to open in prayer and pray for the requests. Whatever the case, I can attest that most years the group meeting has ended up being a source of encouragement and comfort in our daily Christian walk. It's not that prayer is some kind of magical "consecration" of the meeting itself but rather an intentional recognition that all theology is finally conversation not only about God but with God himself.

At the outset of his *Göttingen Dogmatics*, Barth wrote:

> It was significant that Thomas Aquinas put at the head of his *Summa Theologica* the prayer: "Merciful God, I ask that thou wilt grant me, as thou pleases, to seek earnestly, to investigate carefully, to know truthfully, and to present perfectly, to the glory of thy name, amen." If there is any mortally dangerous undertaking on earth, any undertaking in which we have reason not only at the beginning but also in the middle and at the end to take the last resort of invoking the name of the Most High, then it is that of a summa theologica, a dogmatics, and I must add that in our day and in our situation such a prayer will have to be made out of materially much deeper distress and perplexity than in the time of Thomas.[8]

- Finally, recognize that leading a group takes some additional preparation beyond simply reading the assigned text. I try to anticipate some of the barriers that we might face as we are reading the text. For example, if the group does not have access to the Latin translations, I will try to make those translations available. Furthermore, I will usually try to think through two or three questions that can get discussion going. This isn't always easy, and my experience tells me that it doesn't usually take much to get interested participants talking, but being prepared to "prime the pump" can certainly help.

---

[8]Karl Barth, *The Göttingen Dogmatics*, trans. Hannelotte Reiffen (Grand Rapids: Eerdmans, 1991), 3-4.

How to Write a Barth Theology Paper

I have made several assumptions about you, the reader, throughout the course of writing this book, but one is that you are likely at least somewhat aware of the basics of theology and have probably been called on to write some kind of theological or exegetical paper before. If you are one of those people who has never yet written a theology paper, Barth may not be the best theologian on which to cut your theological writing teeth. But then again, why not jump in with both feet?

▶**Resources for Writing Papers:** Although it's not explicitly for teaching people how to write a theology paper, I am convinced that *The Craft of Research* is an excellent general introduction to researching and writing academic papers. Wayne C. Booth, Gregory G. Colomb, and Joseph M. Williams, *The Craft of Research*, 3rd ed. (Chicago: University Of Chicago Press, 2008). For more focused works explicitly on theological research, see Michael Kibbe, *From Topic to Thesis: A Guide to Theological Research* (Downers Grove, IL: IVP Academic, 2016); Robert W. Pazmiño, *Doing Theological Research: An Introductory Guide for Survival in Theological Education* (Eugene, OR: Wipf & Stock, 2009); and Howard Stone and James O. Duke, *How to Think Theologically*, 3rd rev. ed. (Minneapolis: Fortress Press, 2013). For a very short guide, see John M. Frame, *The Doctrine of the Knowledge of God* (Phillipsburg, NJ: P&R Publishing, 1987), 371-74, also available online at http://proginosko.com/docs/frame_theol_paper.html.

If you haven't been explicitly assigned a topic, you will need to decide what kind of paper you want to write. We obviously cannot outline the basics of theological writing here, but I would suggest choosing one of three "tried-and-true" approaches (recognizing that there are many other ways to do it), each of which I present in the form of a question.

Approach #1: What is Barth's position on X? The answer to this question will be an *expository* paper in which you seek to condense into a relatively short paper the most important and salient points that outline Barth's position on a chosen theological topic. Indeed, I tell my students that for the sake of an academic paper, being able to accurately and faithfully represent a theologian's teaching on a matter is far more important than trying to provide a critique or evaluation, especially for beginners. The important task of providing theological critique is a skill that will grow as you mature in your research and thinking. But being a good critical reader means demonstrating first that you are able to present a theologian's position fairly and accurately before seeking to disprove or provide a critical evaluation. Even a profound-sounding critique may be called into question if it can be shown that good exposition has not been accomplished in the first place. To misconstrue a theologian is to commit the theological equivalent of what I call bearing false witness against one's theological neighbor.[9]

As you consider your topic of research, I suggest consulting the *CD*'s index volume as a starting point to see how extensively your topic may have been dealt with and where the most important passages might be found. If you're having trouble deciding on a topic in the first place, then once again, start with the index volume and do some scanning through broad topics of interest to see what you

---

[9]You may be interested in seeing my "Ten Commandments for Theological Students." See https://dguretzki.wordpress.com/pages/10-commandments-for-theological -students.

find. There are innumerable examples that could be given here as topics for consideration—topics as diverse as Barth's position on preaching, biblical authority, the role of the church, his view of the atonement, or even his view on the Catholic teaching about Mary.

Approach #2: How has Barth's position on X changed or remained the same throughout the CD? Answering this type of question will result in a *developmental* paper in which the researcher is looking for consistency and/or change in what Barth says about a particular topic. Keep in mind that change doesn't necessarily mean that Barth takes a *different* position than originally taken (although that could be the case as well) but that he may emphasize certain things later that he does not emphasize earlier.

Although the first (expositional) and second (developmental) types of papers are similar in that both require the researcher to carefully represent what Barth is saying, they differ in respect to what is basically being sought in the exposition. Researchers often call these two respective types of research *synchronic* and *diachronic* methods. That is, a synchronic method seeks to synthesize all the findings and provide a "snapshot" or "bird's-eye" view of the theologian's position at a particular point in time, while a diachronic method seeks to provide an analysis of a theologian's position "through time" and is more akin to a "movie" or a "timeline." A developmental paper will show movements or changes or (in)consistencies (or all three!) in Barth's earlier, middle, and later writings.

Writing a developmental paper could be fruitfully accomplished through comparing an earlier writing of Barth's with a later writing on the same topic. For example, you might be interested in how Barth interprets a particular passage of Scripture such as Romans 5 or John 1. Comparing and contrasting his exegesis of these passages in an early work and a later work can often yield interesting insights into Barth's emphases and theological development.

Alternatively, a developmental paper might examine a topic earlier and later right within the *CD* itself. For example, you might be interested in Barth's perspective on what it means for Jesus Christ to be "begotten" as evidenced in his trinitarian reflections in volume I and in volume IV. Being able to pinpoint and describe those consistencies or changes is the sign of a well-completed developmental research project.

Approach #3: How does Barth's position on X compare with Theologian Z's position on X? The outcome of this kind of question yields the classic *comparative* paper. Comparison and contrast papers are regularly required of undergraduate and graduate students because they force researchers not only to do careful exposition of texts and authors they are reading but also to notice subtle nuances or underlying assumptions that the authors make.

Although there's no reason why a comparison paper cannot be written between any two theologians or exegetes on any given topic, I have found that comparison papers are often (though not always) more likely to yield important insights when the points of comparison are a lot closer to each other rather than radically different. In this regard, Barth sometimes reserved his strongest critique not for those who took radically different positions than himself but for those whose position was much closer (e.g., Emil Brunner). Consequently, a good way to produce a fruitful comparison paper is to begin by noting those with whom Barth regularly interacted, especially in his small-print sections or as revealed in the index. Because Barth was human like us all, it's important for us to read his critiques of others (theologians like Schleiermacher and Bultmann and Przywara are good examples) with a grain of salt and to do our own reading of these individuals with just as much care as we would our reading of Barth, or any other author. That means that a good comparison paper may conclude that Barth's own reading of one of his interlocutors was accurate and fair, or less so. But at any rate, doing a good comparison paper will result in becoming more familiar with other theologians as well. The main temptation to avoid, however, is to start with the intention of taking a stance either to "prove" or "disprove" that Barth was right or wrong about his reading of another theologian. It's rarely that clear-cut, and it's more likely that we will find out that Barth was probably right about many things but, like most humans, not right about other things.

Before I conclude this section on how to write a Barth paper, I want to emphasize that writing a paper on Barth is a daunting task that is complicated by at least three major factors. Even though not all factors can be eliminated, most can be easily mitigated once one becomes aware of them and takes appropriate steps to do so.

Factor 1: The dimensions of Barth's work. Barth's written work is so massive and spread out over so many sources that no one short paper can expect to cover the breadth of what Barth has to say on any given topic. Even if you restricted yourself only to the *CD*, it is likely that Barth has had much to say on any given topic in different places in the various volumes.

In order to deal with this problem, keep in mind two basic strategies: *Limit your investigation to a natural section or portion of the CD and make those limits explicit in your paper.* It is entirely appropriate (and yes, I have seen this done at more scholarly papers and articles than I can count) to indicate that you are going to examine a topic in Barth within only a limited section of the *CD*. To be fair, the limits should not be arbitrarily chosen (e.g., "I'm only going to look at the first 10 pages of the volume") but should represent a natural break in his thought. Often scholars will limit an examination to a single "paragraph," which in the *CD* is meant the sections marked off by the symbol §. In the completed volumes of the *CD*, there are seventy-three so-called paragraphs or sections, not including IV/4 on baptism, which is not demarcated in paragraph form.

Refrain from making grand statements about what Barth defini-tively believes about a topic. This is not to say that you should not state your findings with confidence, but simply remember that it is rarely wise to make a comprehensive statement about Barth's the-ology that a more well-read reader (or professor) will almost cer-tainly be able to refute with counterevidence. That said, do your best to state that *within the constraints of a certain section*, X and Y is indeed what Barth had to say.

Factor 2: The density of Barth's work. If you're reading this book, it's a good chance that you're limited to reading Barth in English translation. And if you have read any Barth at all, you will know how dense his writing can be. His sentences, paragraphs, and sections are long, and he often uses forms of language and ways of speaking that are unfamiliar to English speakers. So what strategy can one use to get past this barrier?

Unfortunately, there is no easy solution. But three things can be kept in mind. First, keep pressing forward. Sometimes beginners get bogged down on a sentence or a term and keep rereading it until they feel they can get it. That may work sometimes, but more often, it is better simply to keep going. Barth has a repetitive style due to the orality underlying the writing of the *CD*, and so if you keep reading, you will likely catch what he's doing, even if you're lost by certain sentences or paragraphs. Second, I have found often that when I get bogged down in Barth's prose it's helpful for me to step back and remind myself where in the structure of the *CD* I find myself. What volume am I reading in? What is the structure of the section as revealed in the table of contents? What sub-heading am I in? What is the opening "bold print" section that is meant to be the guiding statement of the whole section? Third, when you are really stuck, back up to the beginning of a paragraph and read it out loud. (I happen to think this is a good reading strategy for any dif-ficult material.) There is something magical that happens sometimes when we hear the words being spoken that otherwise are trapped in our head. And again, remembering that Barth delivered the *CD* orally can also be good reason to read it out loud, even if it is a translation.

Factor 3: The dialectical nature of Barth's work. If you haven't yet read the entry on **dialectic** in chapter four above, you might want to do that before reading on here. (No, really, go and read it now!)

Welcome back. Because of Barth's dialectical method of doing theology, it is important to understand that one must be very cautious about assuming that what has been said in one section will be definitive for the rest of the work. There are many who have read Barth and have assumed to understand his view on a matter, only to discover that he later takes back or significantly qualifies what he had previously said. Indeed, Barth sometimes seems to contradict himself! (And he may well at times, but just be very sure that he actually is before accusing him of doing so.)

So how do we deal with this feature of Barth's work in a responsible manner? Let me suggest two things. First, take my advice that you should almost *never* say that "Barth always . . ." or "Barth never . . ." because chances are, given the immensity and comprehensiveness of his work, some exception to the rule is possible to be found. This isn't to say that Barth is unpredictable or inconsistent (although he can be both) as much as to say that theological and academic humility recognizes that Barth has usually thought through issues much more thoroughly than most of us are apt to do and thus is cognizant of the complexities we are apt to reduce to bite-sized (or Twitter-lengthed) pieces.

Second, when you do find what appears to be a contradiction or tension in Barth, do not jump immediately to the conclusion that he is making a logical error (although he may be doing exactly that— but sometimes very deliberately!) but ask *why* he is apparently setting two sides of the dialectic against each other. Often Barth upholds the tension precisely in order to accomplish what he hopes: to point away from the statements themselves to the theological reality itself. Barth is convinced, in other words, that truth resides in the object of our inquiry more than in the semantic and verbal meanings of our sentences and paragraphs. So reading Barth recognizing his dialectical commitments will keep you from too quickly seeing contradiction or inconsistency and will press you to consider what, or *who*, he wants us to consider.

For Further Reading

Booth, Wayne C., Gregory G. Colomb, and Joseph M. Williams. *The Craft of Research*. 3rd ed. Chicago: University Of Chicago Press, 2008.

Frame, John M. *The Doctrine of the Knowledge of God*. Phillipsburg, NJ: P&R Publishing, 1987.

Kibbe, Michael. *From Topic to Thesis: A Guide to Theological Research*. Downers Grove, IL: IVP Academic, 2016.

Pazmiño, Robert W. *Doing Theological Research: An Introductory Guide for Survival in Theological Education*. Eugene, OR: Wipf & Stock, 2009.

Stone, Howard, and James O. Duke. *How to Think Theologically*. 3rd rev. ed. Minneapolis: Fortress Press, 2013.

Willimon, William H. *Conversations with Barth on Preaching*. Nashville, TN: Abingdon Press, 2010.

- 8 -

A Guided Tour
of the *Church Dogmatics*

Before embarking on a tour of the *Church Dogmatics*, it's good to become familiar with the print options available in English. As of publication of this book, there are three options for purchasing print editions. (See chapter nine for electronic options.)

Church Dogmatics. Study Edition. 31 volumes. New York: Bloomsbury Publishing, 2009.

The Study Edition of the *CD* includes translations of the Greek, Hebrew, and Latin texts in a paperback format. The downside (and this is a pretty major drawback, in my opinion) is that the page numbers do not align with the original T&T Clark edition (below), which most secondary literature cites.

Church Dogmatics. 14 volumes. New edition. New York: Continuum/ T&T Clark International, 2004.

The new edition of the *CD* reproduces the original T&T Clark edition in hardback, paperback, and PDF formats. The volume quality is high and the text is very readable and retains the original pagination.

Church Dogmatics. 14 volumes. Reprint of original T&T Clark edition. Peabody, MA: Hendrickson, 2010.

This is a good quality hardback reproduction that retains the original T&T Clark typeset and pagination. In my opinion, this set is the best value (read: affordable, yet well bound) available of the *CD*. However, understand that it is a reproduction or copy rather than a brand new typeset, and so there are occasional pages that are of a slightly lower quality of print clarity.

Some Guided Tours of the *Church Dogmatics*

Those who have the privilege of enjoying a hike in a national or state park will be familiar with the various options presented to the hiker. For those who have little experience or time, there is usually an easy option, while more advanced hikers with greater time and experience will have longer and more difficult paths they can follow. Similarly, in this chapter I have laid out three exploratory options for beginning, intermediate, and more advanced (or ambitious) readers of Barth.

Figure 8.1 *Kirchliche Dogmatik*

The **Sampler Track** is designed either for the beginning reader of Barth or for that busy soul who simply needs to get the greatest bang out of her or his reading time. It will cover about 750 pages out of the some 8,500 pages of the *CD*, just under 10 percent. While the person who does this will by no means become an expert Barth reader, completing these pages will provide sufficient exposure to many of his basic theological themes. At about 10-12 pages per day, the Sampler Track could be completed in about six weeks to two months. Alternatively, the Sampler Track could be fruitfully followed in a reading group spread out over a typical semester or term (50-75 pages a week over 10-13 weeks) in academic contexts or in church group settings.

The **Study Track** is an intermediate reading plan that incorporates all the readings from the Sampler Track but adds additional pages or sections to round out the reader's exposure to the *CD*. It covers approximately 1,500 pages of the *CD*, and while it still covers only a small proportion of the whole work (just under 20 percent), the reader, having completed it, will gain some increased confidence in understanding the broader contours of Barth's thought and the larger movements within the *CD* itself. Individually, the Study Track could be completed over the course of a year reading a reasonably manageable pace of about 20 pages per week. The Study Track could also be used in an academic context for an advanced undergraduate or graduate Barth reading course of about 125–150 pages per week over 10-12 weeks.

Finally, I have included a **Scholarly Track** of approximately 2,750 pages, which includes all of the Sampler and Study Track pages plus a significant addition of pages that, if completed, will cover about one third (33 percent) of the *CD*. This could be used as a "slow and steady" option for those who aren't worried about how long their reading will take but who want to be a bit more strategic in their reading other than reading from the first volume through to the last. Or, alternatively, the Scholarly Track could be beneficial for graduate-or doctoral-level students who are not necessarily specializing in Barth but may need to engage him intelligently. I hope that this track will equip readers to become competent commentators on Barth without necessarily having to read the entire *CD*. It would be an ideal track to follow for preparation for a comprehensive exam or as background to thesis research in which Barth is referenced regularly but not as the primary focus.

Experienced hikers know that a good trail guide is not meant to replace the hike itself, nor is the guide meant to reiterate everything that the hiker could possibly see. Rather, a good trail guide prepares the hiker with things to watch for, dangers to avoid, and potential highlights along the way. Similarly, the following guide is incapable of replacing your primary reading. As a guide, it is intended to introduce you to the reading you are about to do as concisely as possible, without giving away what you will find there. For those who want a shortcut—a synopsis or summary quickly available so they do not have to read it themselves—this chapter is sure to disappoint! On the contrary, my goal will be to prepare you *to read,* not do the reading for you. After more than twenty years of reading Barth, I can guarantee you that there is no shortcut to reading him. But I can also guarantee you that careful reading of Barth will either delight or disturb you, but rarely will it bore you.

As far as the format of the reading plans, each section will provide a brief background to what was going on in Barth's life as he wrote that particular section (similar to our ten-stop tour of the pre-*CD* Barth in chapter five above) and a *very* brief summary of major themes in each volume. I then identify some insights into unique features of each volume along with a single statement specially selected from the volume that I believe gets at the "heart" of what Barth is attempting to do. As far as background material, I acknowledge here my indebtedness to Eberhard Busch's biography of Barth for details, though I have not indicated page numbers for each and every detail.

In reference to page numbers, the following convention will be used. A number followed by the letter "a" or "b" indicates that reading should start at the top or bottom half of the page, respectively. The paragraph breaks or beginning or ending points of small/large-print sections should generally make it evident where to begin. Finally, it's important to note that the page numbers refer to the original T&T Clark translation, which is also available through Hendrickson publishers as noted above.

Church Dogmatics I/1—The Doctrine of the Word of God

Background. Barth's first half-volume was published in 1932 while he was serving as a professor of dogmatics at Bonn University in Germany. Barth was forty-six years old at the time. Keep in mind that this was Barth's third attempt to write a dogmatics, with his second attempt (the so-called *Christian Dogmatics*) having been abandoned some five years earlier. Barth had begun to lecture at Bonn in 1930.

Major themes. The first two half-volumes of the *CD* proceed on Barth's assumption that human knowledge of God extends only as far as God has chosen to reveal himself to us, or more precisely, as far as God has chosen to speak to us. Barth calls God's self-revealing the "Word of God," and he seeks in the first two half-volumes to provide his doctrine of the Word of God, a doctrine that corresponds or aligns with the very nature and character of God himself. In the first half-volume, Barth accomplishes three basic things: (1) He defines the task of dogmatics as it relates to the church, arguing that while dogmatics is a unique science of church proclamation, it is a science that does not rest on the assumptions of other human sciences for its justification. (2) He outlines his concept of the threefold Word of God as the Word preached, the Word written, and the Word revealed in Jesus Christ. (3) He sketches out the doctrine of the

Trinity as an outworking of the primal Christian confession "Jesus is Lord." Here he portrays the role of the Father as Creator, the role of the Son as Reconciler, and the role of the Spirit as Redeemer.

Unique feature. There are seventy-three paragraphs (§) in the *CD.* Volume I/1 has twelve paragraphs, or 16 percent of the total number of paragraphs. As Barth wrote, the paragraphs tended to get much longer, so enjoy the relatively short sections in I/1.

CD I/1 in a nutshell. "God reveals Himself as the Lord; [this] we call the root of the doctrine of the Trinity" (*CD* I/1, 397).

Table 8.1. *Church Dogmatics* I/1—*The Doctrine of the Word of God*

Sampler		Study		Scholarly	
Read	Total Pages	Read	Total Pages	Read	Total Pages
Preface, xi-xvii	7	Preface, xi-xvii	7	Preface, xi-xvii	7
88-94a	7	3-24	22	3-24	22
99-104	6	88-120	33	47-71	25
111-120	10	304-333	30	88-124	37
304-315a	12	399-409a	11	304-383	80
				384-390	7
				399-409a	11
				448-466	19
Total	42		103		208

Church Dogmatics I/2—The Doctrine of the Word of God

Background. The second half-volume was almost twice as long as the first and was not published until 1938, a full six years later. This was a tumultuous and no doubt distracting time for Barth. It was between the half-volumes that Barth wrote the Barmen Declaration (1934), penned his famous *"Nein!"* essay in response to Brunner, and was dismissed from his post at Bonn after refusing to swear an unconditional oath to Hitler. Barth moved back to Basel, Switzerland, his hometown, in 1935, where he took up teaching at the university. This was where Barth spent the remainder of his teaching career, and indeed, the remainder of his life.

Major themes. Barth carried forward the second and third parts of his doctrine of revelation begun in *CD* I/1. Whereas in the first half he spoke of revelation through the lens of the doctrine of the Trinity, in I/2 he specifically focused on revelation from the perspective of Christology (most specifically the incarnation of the Word) and from the perspective of pneumatology (most specifically the outpouring of the Holy Spirit on the church). In the pneumatological section, Barth clarifies his understanding of how God's Word stands in dialectical relationship to religion.[1] He follows this up with a major exploration of his doctrine of Scripture (chapter three) and the mission of the church as the people of the Spirit called out to proclaim God's Word to herself and to the world.

Unique feature. *CD* I/2 is the longest part volume of the whole *CD*, reaching 990 pages in German and 884 pages in English.

Table 8.2. *Church Dogmatics I/2—The Doctrine of the Word of God*

Sampler		Study		Scholarly	
Read	Total Pages	Read	Total Pages	Read	Total Pages
14-25	11	1-25	25	1-25	25
172-184	13	172-196	25	80-101	22
297b-303a	6	280-309	30	147-171	25
307b-309	3	323-325	3	172-184	12
323-325	3	457-476	20	280-325	46
457-465	9	481-492a	11	457-476	20
473-476	4			481-496	16
481-486	6			661-673	12
				695-713b	19
Total	**55**		**114**		**197**

---

[1]On Barth's understanding the relationship of revelation and religion, see **abolition** in chapter 4.

CD I/2 in a nutshell. "That the Word became 'flesh' . . . this consummation of God's condescension, this inconceivability which is greater than the inconceivability of the divine majesty and the inconceivability of human darkness put together: this is the revelation of the Word of God" (*CD* I/2, 152).

Church Dogmatics II/1—The Doctrine of God

Background. Published in 1940 at the outset of World War II, *CD* II/1 marks the first half of Barth's extensive doctrine of God. During this time Barth appears to have become much more adept at preparing lectures and writing his dogmatics, even while paying special attention to the critical political matters that concerned the whole populace. Living in neutral Switzerland did not mean for Barth political passivity but an active commitment to political resistance to being caught up in the European theater of war. Just as this volume was about to come to press, Barth reported for armed military service, at age 54, in defense of the homeland. Although these historical elements do not show up very often in Barth's prose, it is noteworthy how confidently Barth proclaimed the reality of God in the midst of a time when God probably seemed to be either absent or very distant. It is very likely that Barth was at the peak of his scholarly productivity at this time.

Major themes. *CD* II/1 has two major chapters "The Knowledge of God" and "The Reality of God." In the first chapter, Barth sets up a dialectic of knowledge that moves from the human's place before God to God's place before humans, followed up with a second dialectic of God's readiness for humanity and humanity's readiness for God. Most fundamentally, Barth identifies the incarnation of Jesus Christ as the very place at which knowledge of God can be gained. God is knowable to humans only because he has actively and incarnately (and not just cognitively) given himself to be known as a man among humans.

In the second chapter, Barth seeks to close the gap that theologians have often set between the "being" and the "becoming" of

God. According to Barth, God's existence (his being) is united with and fully aligned with his action (his becoming) so that to know God in his "is-ness" is to know God through his actions. Barth works out in this section his doctrine of divine perfections (rather than the traditional "attributes"). Here Barth carefully qualifies that the descriptors used for God (goodness, holiness, faithfulness, etc.) are unique to God alone and thus, properly speaking, apply fully and directly to God alone and to his creatures only indirectly by analogy. It is only to God that these traditionally labeled attributes "perfectly" apply. For this reason, Barth calls these descriptors the perfections of God.

Unique feature. *CD* II/1 is one of the few volumes that contains a fascinating autobiographical section in which Barth sets his own theological project in the context of the history that went before him and in which he found himself. The autobiographical element can be found on pages 633-638. I have included this section in all three tracks.

Table 8.3. *Church Dogmatics* II/1—*The Doctrine of God*

Sampler		Study		Scholarly	
Read	Total Pages	Read	Total Pages	Read	Total Pages
3-10	8	3-18	16	3-53	51
31b-38	7	31b-53	23	63-79	17
272b-281	10	63-72	10	179-204	26
322-327	6	179-186	8	257-287	36
351-363	13	257-263	7	322-350	29
440-447	8	272b-287	16	440-461	22
633-638	6	322-327	6	608-619	12
		330-335	6	633-649	16
		440-447	8		
		608-619	12		
		633-638	6		
Total	**58**		**118**		**209**

CD II/1 in a nutshell. "God is who He is in the act of His revelation" (*CD* II/1, 257).

Church Dogmatics II/2—The Doctrine of God

Background. Two years passed between the first and second halves of Barth's *Doctrine of God.* In 1942 Barth published II/2, a volume that many have hailed as one of Barth's crowning achievements—his reworking of the traditional Reformed doctrine of election. At the time, Barth had resettled into being professor of dogmatics in Basel, Switzerland, and had made new acquaintances, probably most significantly the Jesuit theologian Hans Urs von Balthasar, who eventually wrote an important interpretation of Barth's theology. Of course, the war had dragged on, keeping everyone on edge. But death struck closer to home when in June 1940, he lost his brother Peter, a Calvin scholar. To make matters worse, a year later, again in June, Barth's twenty-year-old son Matthias was killed in a mountain climbing accident. Nevertheless, in March 1941, Barth was delighted to receive a visit from Dietrich Bonhoeffer, the young theologian who was eventually executed for treason under Hitler just before the end of the war. From Bonhoeffer, Barth received a firsthand account of what was happening in Germany and, perhaps most importantly, some of the troubling reports of what was taking place in regard to the brutal persecution of Jews in Germany.

Major themes. The most famous topic for which *CD* II/2 is known is Barth's reconceptualization of the doctrine of election (chapter seven), but he also dealt with the question of ethics as an outworking of a proper doctrine of God (chapter eight). Regarding election, Barth made the radical proposal that it was to be understood as the very core of the gospel itself. He challenged the traditional Reformed doctrines of election that tended to place election under the topic of God's hidden eternal decrees, and instead proposed that God's election is made fully known in the person of Jesus Christ. Rather than beginning with the idea of God's pre-temporal selection of individuals for eternal salvation or damnation, Barth instead identified Jesus Christ as both the Electing God and the Elected Man, the Subject and Object of election. Only after having understood Christ's centrality to election was it then possible to speak of the election of the community (which for Barth included both Israel and the church in a dialectical relationship in which the two served as negative and positive witnesses to Christ, respectively), and then and only then to speak of the election of the individual.

As for Barth's chapter on ethics, Barth argued that God's commands to humanity were preeminent in making ethical decisions. However, God's commands must be understood in light of God's election of humans to be in covenant with him. Thus, there is no such thing, according to Barth, as an ethics isolated from God's electing grace. On the contrary, all humans, whether in the church or not, are claimed by God as his holy possession, all are measured in their actions by God against the standard of his Son, and all are ultimately judged righteous by God in and through the provision of his Son's death and resurrection.

Unique feature. We noted earlier that Barth's doctrine of election is unique in the history of theology, but it is doubly unique insofar as Barth makes God's covenant of election in Christ the basis for ethics rather than the providential will and law of God that had been a more typical basis for ethics in the Protestant and Catholic traditions.

CD II/2 in a nutshell. "There is no such thing as a will of God apart from the will of Jesus Christ" (*CD* II/2, 115).

Table 8.4. *Church Dogmatics II/2—The Doctrine of God*

Sampler		Study		Scholarly	
Read	Total Pages	Read	Total Pages	Read	Total Pages
94-99	6	3-10	8	3-10	8
103-106	4	34-41	8	34-41	8
115-117	3	94-106	13	76-106	31
120-127	8	115-145	31	115-145	31
195-201	12	195-205	11	195-213	18
306-325	19	306-325	20	233-240	8
		340-354	15	306-356b	51
		543-551	9	393-404a	12
				410-419	10
				509-513	5
				543-551	9
				733-741	9
Total	**52**		**115**		**200**

Church Dogmatics III/1—The Doctrine of Creation

Background. Barth embarked on his doctrine of creation in the third volume of his *CD* and released the first part near the end of the war in 1945. During its composition, the war was raging on. Barth continued to send letters of encouragement (and resistance) to Christians suffering under terrible conditions in various locales. Sometimes these letters were even smuggled in on microfilm. Despite the circumstances, Barth pressed on, with Mozart often playing in the background as he wrote. Given the circumstances surrounding the beginnings of his work on the doctrine of creation, his words in the preface of the first part volume were revealing:

> In taking up the doctrine of creation I have entered a sphere in
> which I feel much less confident and sure. If I were not obliged
> to do so in the course of my general exposition of Church dog-

matics, I should probably not have given myself so soon to a detailed treatment of this particular material.[2] But we can be grateful that Barth pressed forward because his resulting doctrine of creation, extending over four parts, constitutes one of the most expansive doctrines of creation ever written.

Major themes. *CD* III/1 contains a single chapter, which Barth titled "The Work of Creation," covered in three paragraphs: §40. Faith in God the Creator; §41. Creation and Covenant; and §42. The Yes of God the Creator. From these paragraphs, three major themes in Barth's doctrine of creation emerge. First, Barth insists that the doctrine of creation can be confessed only by faith in God. That is, one cannot examine or study the world and conclude from such examination that God is the Creator. Rather, it is only by God's gracious revelation of himself to humanity that it can be known and confessed that humans do in fact exist to be covenant partners with God in the good world he has created. Second, Barth argues that creation itself—the heavens and the earth—are to be understood as the theatre of God's covenantal dealings with humanity, a covenantal relationship established and revealed in the God-man, Jesus Christ. Creation is the external outworking of God's covenant, and God's covenant is the inner rationality of creation. Third, Barth carefully lays out how God himself gives his affirmation—his Yes—to humanity through the creation, noting that the world as God created it is designed for human benefit. Creation is the context or theater in which humans have been placed to live life before God.

Unique feature. A major portion of this volume is taken up with a theological exposition/exegesis of the first two chapters of Genesis. After giving careful attention to the nature of these chapters, which Barth designates as *saga* (rather than history, myth,

---

[2]*CD* III/1, ix.

or legend), Barth engages in a breathtaking retelling of the Genesis creation accounts—a retelling that takes up over 130 pages of text.

CD III/1 in a nutshell. "God in Himself is neither deaf nor dumb but speaks and hears His Word from all eternity, so outside His eternity He does not wish to be without hearing or echo, that is, without the ears and voices of the creature" (50).

Table 8.5. *Church Dogmatics* III/1—*The Doctrine of Creation*

Sampler		Study		Scholarly	
Read	Total Pages	Read	Total Pages	Read	Total Pages
3-22a	20	3-22a	20	3-41	39
63-65	3	59-69	11	59-99	41
80-84	5	80-99	20	176-206	31
90b-94	5	184b-191	8	228-266	39
330-334	5	228-239	12	330-388	59
344-350	7	330-350	21		
366-375	10	366-388	23		
Total	**55**		**115**		**209**

Church Dogmatics III/2—The Doctrine of Creation

Background. According to Barth's own testimony in his preface to III/2, the volume was delayed in publication until 1948 both because Barth had found himself in a very busy time and also because he was being extra cautious about what he was writing. Of great concern to him was that the exegesis of the many biblical texts he was dealing with was completed responsibly, especially because he discerned the novelty of what he was suggesting. Indeed, Barth speculated that III/2 was more theologically novel in the context of the history of theology than even his doctrine of election in II/2. By the time he wrote his preface, Barth's confidence levels had risen significantly from the time he had launched into the doctrine of creation. This is evidenced by his confident remark that the "theological doctrine of man [anthropology] proposed here is not only possible, but the only one possible" (!) (ix).

By now we need to remember that history itself had changed significantly: although World War II was over, the world found itself in the atomic age after the dropping of the first atomic bombs in Japan. This reality undoubtedly weighed heavily on Barth, particularly as he sought to work out his anthropology in such a way that he acknowledged the reality of human sin even while seeking to speak about the glory of humanity called to be imaged in the likeness of Jesus Christ.

Major themes. *CD* III/2 is a massive volume devoted to the singular theme of "The Creature" or more specifically, the doctrine of humanity (anthropology). Barth devotes five paragraphs (§43-§47) to unpacking his anthropology. After doing a survey of the theological history of anthropology (§43), Barth deals with the human as creature (§44), as a covenant partner with God (§45), as an enfleshed-soul (§46), and finally as one with a unique time (§47). Not surprisingly, Barth worked out these aspects of anthropology through the lens of Christology, with Jesus of Nazareth representing the human for all other humans ("Jesus, Man for Other Men"). Jesus Christ, in other words, is the true pattern by which all other human existence can be understood and lived.

Unique feature. Although there are several unique facets to Barth's anthropology, Barth's discussion of the relationship of God's time to human time in §47 is one of the most theologically pertinent discussions paralleling advances in twentieth-century physics and Einstein's reconfiguration of our understanding of time. In II/1 Barth stated what he understood to be the problem: "The theological concept of eternity must be set free from the Babylonian captivity of an abstract opposite to the concept of time" (*CD* II/1, 611). Thus in III/2 Barth seeks to provide his own solution to the problem: "God also lives in His time. But his time is eternity, which has no fixed span, no margins, no other measure but Himself. Eternity is not time without beginning or end. Time is the mode of existence of the creature" (*CD* III/2, 558).[3]

CD III/2 in a nutshell. "If the divinity of the man Jesus is to be described comprehensively in the statement that He is man for God, His humanity can and must be described no less succinctly in the proposition that He is man for man, for other men, His fellows" (208).

Table 8.6. *Church Dogmatics* III/2—*The Doctrine of Creation*

Sampler		Study		Scholarly	
Read	Total Pages	Read	Total Pages	Read	Total Pages
55-61a	7	19-28	9	3-28	26
203-214	12	55-71	17	55-71	17
325-332	8	203-222	20	203-222	20
437-456	20	325-344	20	325-344	20
		344-356	13	344-356	13
		437-466	29	437-466	29
		511b-522	12	511b-522	12
				553b-572	20
				572-587	16
				587-613	27
Total	**47**		**120**		**200**

Church Dogmatics III/3—The Doctrine of Creation

Background. A new decade dawned in 1950 with the publication of the third part of Barth's doctrine of creation. Keep in mind that by now, Barth was sixty-four years old and had reached only the halfway point of the *CD*. It was also the beginning of the Cold War era and communist expansion, and the time of the official division

---

[3]For a helpful analysis of Barth's understanding of the relationship between time and eternity, see Adrian Langdon, *God the Eternal Contemporary* (Eugene, OR: Wipf & Stock, 2012).

of Germany into its Eastern and Western sectors. Although Barth remained busy, at least one event associated with the writing of III/3 is notable. In December of 1949, Barth gave a talk on Swiss radio, "The Jewish Question and Its Christian Answer," which was a distillation and simplified version of a section from III/3 (most likely pages 210-226). It opened up the way for Barth to meet with religious Jews in Basel and for ongoing conversation with the Jewish scholar Martin Buber, whom Barth grew to admire greatly.

Major themes. Barth's third part volume on creation has some of the most far-ranging themes, moving from his discussion of the doctrine of providence (§48), to the concept of God's lordship (§49), to the problem of evil and nothingness (§50), and finally to his discussion of angels and their "opponents," the demonic (§51). Yet as diverse as these topics seem, this volume can be understood essentially as Barth's theology of the kingdom of God. For whether it's in the general history and outworking of the visible physical world or the invisible world of strange spiritual realities of which we know so little, Barth is adamant: "The King Himself has come; He has brought a sacrifice for His people, and in this way He has demonstrated Himself to be the Victor" (181).

Unique feature. Hands down, Barth's discussion of nothingness stands out in this volume. It is his attempt to describe rationally the irrationality of the potential and reality of evil in God's created world. The difficulty of the topic is reflected in one of his section titles: "The Reality of Nothingness" (See **nothingness** in chapter four above.)

CD III/3 in a nutshell. "What God wills as He works 'all in all' (1 Cor. 12:6), and what He therefore works, is that His free grace should be radiant, and take form, and conquer and rule in the creaturely world" (33).

Table 8.7. *Church Dogmatics III/3—The Doctrine of Creation*

Sampler		Study		Scholarly	
Read	Total Pages	Read	Total Pages	Read	Total Pages
33b-40	8	33b-57	25	3-14	12
239-246	8	239-246	8	33b-57	25
289-295	7	265b-288	24	58-70	13
349-356	8	349-356	8	90b-107a	18
369-373	5	356-368	13	154b-162	9
477-486	10	369-373	5	239-288	49
519-531	13	418-428a	11	349-368	20
		477-486	10	369-380	12
		519-531	13	418-441	24
				477-486	10
				519-531	13
Total	**59**		**117**		**205**

Church Dogmatics III/4—The Doctrine of Creation

Background. In honor of Barth's sixty-fourth birthday, the American Academy of Arts and Sciences in Boston appointed him as a Foreign Honorary Member. In gratitude, Barth dedicated III/4 to the Academy.[4] By the time the volume was published in 1951, Barth was sixty-five years old.

Major themes. Barth completed his doctrine of creation as he typically did at the end of each volume—with attention to the question of ethics: What do the realities of God as Creator and humans as his creatures mean for their lives lived before him? Barth focuses his answer on the theme of freedom. According to Barth, God created his special creatures, man and woman, to enjoy a

---

[4]The dedicatory page does not show up in the English translation. The dedication reads: *"Der American Academy of Arts and Sciences in Boston (Massachusetts) als Zeichen des Dankes."* ("To the American Academy of Arts and Sciences in Boston (Massachusetts) as a sign of gratitude.")

relative (though not absolute) degree of freedom before God, a freedom appropriate to them as creatures. Barth discusses humanity's freedom before God (§53); their freedom before each other in fellowship (§54); their freedom to respect, protect, and enjoy life itself (§55); and their freedom to enact their life before God in the unique circumstances and callings particular to their time and place in history (§56)—a freedom of limitation, Barth calls it. Most importantly for the entire volume, Barth lays out his understanding of ethics in such a way that he avoids making ethics into a life lived following rules (casuistry) in favor of living daily in obedience to God. This meant, for Barth, an obedience to a living, speaking God through active listening to his Word and Command within the context of the church and within the particular context and history in which it is heard.

Unique feature. This is the longest of the four parts in the doctrine of creation. The German text ran 789 pages (685 in English), just a tad longer than III/2, which was 780 pages.

CD III/4 in a nutshell. "The God who meets man as Creator in His commandment is the God 'who is gracious to him in Jesus Christ.' He is not, then, a new and strange God who could require from man as his Commander something new and strange and even perhaps in conflict with what is asked of him by the God who is gracious to him in Jesus Christ" (35).

Table 8.8. *Church Dogmatics* III/4—*The Doctrine of Creation*

Sampler		Study		Scholarly	
Read	Total Pages	Read	Total Pages	Read	Total Pages
47-58	12	47-58	12	3-19	17
163-172	10	73-86	14	47-72	26
450-470	21	116-129	14	73-86	14
595-600	6	163-172	10	87-97	11
		240b-249a	10	116-141	26
		324-332	9	163-199	37
		450-470a	21	240b-249b	10
		470-484	15	285-298a	14
		595-600	6	324-337	14
				450-470a	21
				470-484	15
				595-600	6
Total	**49**		**111**		**211**

Church Dogmatics IV/1, 2, and 3, *The Doctrine of Reconciliation*

Background. With the massive doctrine of creation now finished, Barth turned his attention to what might appropriately be identified as the heart and climax of the *CD*: the doctrine of reconciliation. Barth had originally considered developing the fourth volume as the doctrine of the covenant, thus aligning it more closely with the doctrine of creation he had just completed. In the end, however, he stuck to the originally planned title of "reconciliation." Although it's only speculation, I do wonder whether reconciliation rung more practically true to Barth in the context of the various controversies in which he was implicated. Given that the Cold War divide between East and West had been increasingly evident, Barth was challenged by some of his critics to come out more harshly not only against the communist regimes of the East but also the capitalist regimes headed by the United States in the West. Despite the increased postwar militarization taking place around the world, Barth refused to take a pacifist stand but simultaneously refused to support increased militarization. Barth's theme of "reconciliation," although primarily meant to be a theology of reconciliation between God and humanity, was a theme that was much needed in the time in which Barth wrote in the 1950s.

In the end, Barth's doctrine of reconciliation proper remains incomplete but also represents the largest of the four volumes. Fragments of the unfinished portion were eventually published under the separate title of *The Christian Life*. In many respects, volume IV stands as a "dogmatics within the dogmatics" because, as we will shortly see, it covered nearly the whole breadth of the traditional topics of theology, from the doctrine of the Trinity to eschatology.

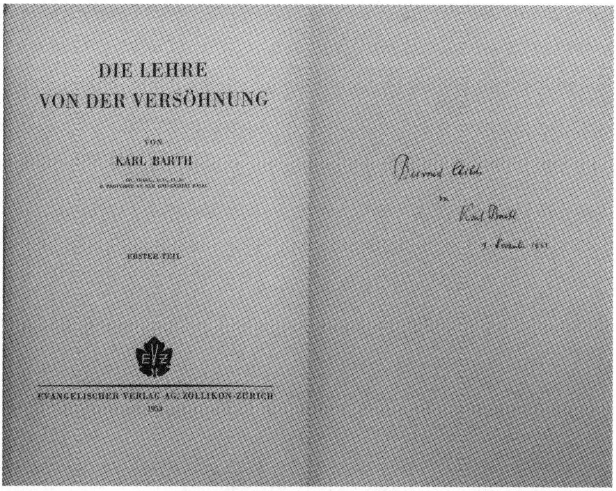

Figure 8.2. Autographed copy of *KD* IV/1 to Brevard Childs. Author's collection.

Major themes. I have opted to deal with the first three parts of the doctrine of reconciliation together because seeing their interrelation is so much more important here than in any other part of the *CD*. While in previous volumes Barth was able to deal with his subject matter in a slightly more linear fashion, following a topic through in a straight line, the doctrine of reconciliation pushed Barth to think more synthetically and in a nonlinear fashion. At one level, the doctrine of reconciliation is really the essence of Barth's Christology, but it is also his soteriology. This was intentional for Barth because he was so convinced that Jesus Christ couldn't be spoken of in isolation or abstraction from who he is as the Savior of the world. Jesus Christ is known, in other words, precisely and most fully by what he does—through providing salvation to humanity. And in providing that salvation, Barth also tries to speak to the destiny or calling humans have received as the people of God—a people gathered, built, and sent by the Holy Spirit in its mission to the world. Thus, there is a sense in which Barth tries to unpack his Christology, soteriology, and ecclesiology all at the same time. Therefore, for readers to really get what he was doing, it is necessary to understand Barth's vision for the whole right at the outset.

Given the somewhat new approach that he takes in volume IV, Barth decides to provide an overview, contained in §58, of the whole doctrine of reconciliation he has planned. There he identifies the three forms of the doctrine of reconciliation he intends to present, three forms that bring together his Christology and his soteriology. They are (1) the humiliation of Jesus the man ("Jesus Christ, the Lord as Servant"), (2) the exaltation of Jesus ("Jesus Christ, the Servant as Lord"), and (3) the call of Jesus ("Jesus Christ, the True Witness"). The threefold form of reconciliation simultaneously intends to say something about Jesus Christ and about what Jesus Christ accomplishes. Consequently, the three forms of the doctrine of Christ correspond to the three forms of salvation that Barth identifies as the doctrines of justification (found in IV/1), sanctification (found in IV/2), and vocation (found in IV/3).

Finally, we note that each of the first three parts of IV are intentionally structured in (beautiful!) parallel. The pattern for each part is as follows: christology, anthropology/sin, soteriology, pneumatology/ecclesiology, and ethics. This order represents respectively Barth's overarching commitments to (1) the priority of Christology for all of theology, (2) an understanding of humanity's sin as being a breaching of their covenant status before God and an antithesis (or "anti-Christ") to what Christ represents, (3) an understanding of salvation as a "benefit" of God's covenant with humans in Jesus Christ, (4) seeing the outworking of God's covenant as being primarily manifest in the spiritual people of God and the church, and (5) the outworking of the church's life in obedience to God's command revealed in Jesus Christ. I believe there is no better way to understand this structure than to visualize it as in table 8.9.

Table 8.9. The structure of Barth's *Doctrine of Reconciliation* (volume IV)

	CD IV/1	**CD IV/2**	**CD IV/3**
Christology	Christ's *Obedience* §59	Christ's *Exaltation* §64	Christ's *Glory* §69
Anthropology/Sin	Human *Pride* §60	Human *Sloth* and *Misery* §65	Human *Falsehood* §70
Soteriology	*Justification* §61	*Sanctification* §66	*Vocation* §71
Pneumatology/ Ecclesiology	The Spirit's *Gathering* of the Community §62	The Spirit's *Upbuilding* of the Community §67	The Spirit's *Sending* of the Community §72
Ethics	The Spirit and Christian *Faith* §63	The Spirit and Christian *Love* §68	The Spirit and Christian *Hope* §73

CD IV/1 in a nutshell. "God re-establishes the covenant, or rather, He maintains and continues it, in order to lead to his goal the man whom He has brought into covenant with Him" (79).

CD IV/2 in a nutshell. "As God condescends and humbles Himself to man and becomes man, man himself is exalted, not as God or like God, but to God, being placed at His side, not in identity, but in true fellowship with Him, and becoming a new man in this exaltation and fellowship" (6).

CD IV/3.1 & IV/3.2 in a nutshell. "Jesus Christ as attested to us in Holy Scripture is the one Word of God whom we must hear and whom we must trust and obey in life and in death" (IV/3.1, 3).[5]

Table 8.10. *Church Dogmatics IV/1—The Doctrine of Reconciliation*

Sampler		Study		Scholarly	
Read	Total Pages	Read	Total Pages	Read	Total Pages
79-154	75	3-18a	16	3-18a	16
		79-154	75	79-154	75
		157-174	18	157-192	36
		413-423	11	211-224	14
		643-650	8	283-295a	13
		725-739	15	358-366	9
				413-432	20
				478-486a	9
				514-521	8
				643-650	8
				725-739	15
				740-755	16
Total	**75**		**143**		**239**

---

[5]Barth's opening thesis to IV/3 is taken verbatim from the text of the Barmen Declaration written in 1934. For the text of the Barmen Declaration, see www.sacred-texts.com/chr/barmen.htm. For a relatively recent commentary on Barmen, see Eberhard Busch and Daniel Migliore, *The Barmen Theses Then and Now: The 2004 Warfield Lectures at Princeton Theological Seminary*, trans. Darrell Guder and Judith Guder (Grand Rapids: Eerdmans, 2010).

Table 8.11. *Church Dogmatics* IV/2—*The Doctrine of Reconciliation*

Sampler		Study		Scholarly	
Read	Total Pages	Read	Total Pages	Read	Total Pages
156-166	11	154b-166	13	3-20	18
264-274	11	264-282	19	31-36	6
403-409	7	403-409	7	154b-192	39
499-511a	13	499-511a	13	264-306	43
533-553	21	533-553	21	378-403	26
623-630	8	623-641	19	403-424	22
783-795a	13	783-803	21	499-511a	13
				533-553	21
				623-641	19
				783-824	45
Total	**84**		**113**		**252**

Table 8.12. *Church Dogmatics* IV/3.1—*The Doctrine of Reconciliation*

Sampler		Study		Scholarly	
Read	Total Pages	Read	Total Pages	Read	Total Pages
48b-64	17	38b-75	38	3-38	36
261-274	14	165-171	7	38b-86	49
362-367	6	261-274	14	165-191	27
368-378a	11	362-367	6	261-274	14
434-446	13	368-388	21	274b-281a	8
		434-453	20	362-367	6
				368-397	30
				434-453	20
				461b-478	18
Total	**61**		**106**		**208**

Table 8.13. *Church Dogmatics* IV/3.2—*The Doctrine of Reconciliation*

Sampler		Study		Scholarly	
Read	Total Pages	Read	Total Pages	Read	Total Pages
490b-497	8	486-497	12	481-497	17
497b-504	8	497-510a	14	497-514	18
526-531a	6	520b-534	15	520b-554a	35
571-576	6	571-592a	22	554-592	39
769-784	16	769-784	16	769-795	27
795b-801	7	795b-809a	15	795b-830	36
872-878	7	864b-878	15	864b-901	38
Total	**58**		**109**		**210**

Church Dogmatics IV/4—*The Doctrine of Reconciliation* (Fragment)

Background. The last volume included with the *CD* does not technically extend Barth's doctrine of reconciliation as he originally planned. By the mid-1960s, Barth had slowed considerably in carrying out his writing, but he had a surge of activity in the winter of 1966 and 1967 when he produced this volume on his views on baptism. As it turned out, Barth's arguments developed against the practice of infant baptism were and have been controversial, with some seeing Barth's final volume as being out of line not only with the Reformed tradition generally but with his own thinking developed in the *CD*. On the other hand, other theologians have argued that Barth's conclusions in IV/4 are a natural outworking of the trajectory of Barth's ecclesiology already hinted at and developed in earlier volumes.[6] As for the primary influence by which Barth arrived at his conclusions, Barth gives credit to his oldest son

---

[6]For the most recent review of the scholarship on Barth's doctrine of baptism as represented in IV/4, see W. Travis McMaken, *The Sign of the Gospel* (Minneapolis, MN: Fortress Press, 2013).

and New Testament scholar, Markus, for his book calling into question the sacramental nature of baptism.[7]

It should be noted that the paragraphs in IV/4 are not numbered as in the previous volumes, indicating that the volume is, strictly speaking, an unfinished fragment, not a continuation of the originally planned sequence.

Major themes. Barth's sole topic in IV/4 is the doctrine of baptism, but he unfolds his exposition in two parts: "Baptism with the Holy Spirit" and "Baptism with Water." Barth argues that the beginning of the Christian life is initiated solely by the Holy Spirit. Barth designates this starting point of the Christian life baptism by the Holy Spirit. However, he goes on to argue that the first step of obedience and faithfulness of the Christian life corresponding to the Spirit's initiation is the baptism by water, an action that a human freely decides and requests from the church. As a corresponding human action to the Spirit's action (see **correspondence** in chapter four), water baptism according to Barth is strictly a response to God's grace but not a "means of grace" (to use standard sacramental language). As Barth noted, "I had to abandon the 'sacramental' understanding of baptism, which I still maintained fundamentally in 1943."[8]

Unique feature. CD IV/4 is the shortest of all the volumes (only 213 pages of text in English) but also has the reputation of being the most controversial among both Barth's sympathizers and his critics.

CD IV/4 in a nutshell. "[Water baptism] is a public declaration on the part of the [Spirit-] baptised that they stand in a personal relation to the Lord of the Christian community as the only source and cause of all salvation" (83).

---

[7]Markus Barth, *Die Taufe—ein Sakrament?: Ein exegetischer Beitrag zum Gespräch über die kirchliche Taufe* (Zollikon-Zürich: Evang. Verl., 1951).
[8]*CD* IV/4, x.

Table 8.14. *Church Dogmatics* IV/4—*The Doctrine of Reconciliation* (fragment)

Sampler		Study		Scholarly	
Read	Total Pages	Read	Total Pages	Read	Total Pages
vii-xii	6	vii-xii	6	vii-xii	6
3-23	21	3-40	38	3-213	211
50-61	12	50-100	51		
68-90	23	130-148	19		
Total	**62**		**114**		**217**

- 9 -

For Further Exploration

One of my primary goals in writing this little book was to get people to take more time to read Barth for themselves and rely less on secondary assessments and commentary. I hope that you will take the plunge and read more Barth, and in turn, be driven back to read more Bible. In fact, may I suggest that you make a commitment that the more Barth you read, the more you will also read Holy Scripture? If you do that, I have a feeling that Barth would be happy. And I think the Lord will be pleased, too.

That said, this little book has been written with full awareness that at some point we all need a little help from some expert guides who can help us understand the "twentieth-century church father" just a little bit better. In what follows, I provide three lists of key resources that may be helpful to those entering the realm of Barth studies. The first list is meant to serve those at the introductory level, and the second list is a select group of texts that will take you into a more intermediate level of insights. The third list points readers to other kinds of resources that are available for delving deeper into the world of Barth scholarship.

Please note that I have intentionally *not* included an advanced list of secondary sources because there are simply so many works available that it would be impossible to keep the list short. If you are already at the advanced level, you should be able to find such books on your own, or at least peruse some of the footnotes throughout this book where I've made mention of some of these works. However, if you want to get a good sense of the titles that might make the advanced list, I'd recommend taking a look at the Routledge/Ashgate Barth Studies series[1] and the T&T Clark Studies in Systematic Theology series,[2] both of which have a good variety of scholarly works on Barth.

Introductory Sources

Busch, Eberhard. *Karl Barth: His Life from Letters and Autobiographical Texts*. Grand Rapids: Eerdmans, 1976.

Eberhard Busch was Karl Barth's last research assistant, who also lived for a time at the Barth residence. Busch's book is the most extensive biography of Barth we have and is the text I have cited frequently throughout this guide. Busch masterfully weaves biography and theology together in a work unlikely to be paralleled any time soon. For those who want to delve into the details of Barth's life as illustrated from primary sources (such as Barth's own letters and papers), Busch is sure to delight and inform.

Busch, Eberhard. *Barth*. Nashville: Abingdon Press, 2008.

Busch has more recently penned a short theological introduction to the entire scope of Barth's theology, and he is the only author who gets two works listed here! I know of no other equal to the accomplishment of this little ninety-five-page work. The wonderful thing is that you can read it slowly and savor its insights. Truly great for the beginner!

Jüngel, Eberhard. *Karl Barth. A Theological Legacy*. Trans. Garrett E. Paul. Philadelphia, PA: Westminster Press, 1986.

It's unfortunate that this book is out of print, but you should be able to access it in a library or find it used online. Jüngel's book provides

---

[1]For a full list of titles, see www.routledge.com/series/ABARTH.
[2]See www.bloomsbury.com/us/series/tt-clark-studies-in-systematic-theology.

an overview of Barth's life and work, an assessment of his early theological career, and at a slightly more advanced level, his interpretation of the "interpretations" of Barth. Included in this volume is Jüngel's tribute written after Barth's death in 1968.

Torrance, Thomas F. *Karl Barth, Biblical and Evangelical Theologian*. Edinburgh: T & T Clark, 1990.

T. F. Torrance was the chief editor of the English translation of Karl Barth's *CD* (as well as Calvin's New Testament commentaries, we might add). Although a noteworthy theologian in his own right, Torrance was closely acquainted with Barth and is one of the most important English interpreters of his work. This book is a great mix of theological and biographical insight into Barth the theologian and biblical exegete.

Webster, John B. *Barth's Earlier Theology: Four Studies*. New York: T&T Clark, 2005.

Webster's book is perhaps a bit beyond introductory but still very accessible. He focuses on the earlier exegetical and historical works of Barth and makes an argument for how those shaped the direction of his later theology. Webster is convinced that too often philosophical and cultural interpretations of Barth have failed to see how important Barth's own exegesis of Scripture and his positioning within the Reformed tradition were for his theological development.

Intermediate Sources

Balthasar, Hans Urs von. *The Theology of Karl Barth: Exposition and Interpretation*. New York: 1971; San Francisco: Ignatius Press, 1992.

Hans Urs von Balthasar was a Swiss Catholic colleague of Barth's at Basel. Balthasar's book provides a distinct and powerful interpretation of Barth but is also an intensive work of ecumenical dialogue. Although some aspects of Bathasar's interpretation of Barth's theological development have been challenged in the past two decades, his work still stands as a classic and has significant insights into Barth's emphases and themes. Unfortunately, Balthasar's book is more often spoken about in Barth circles but less often actually read. Don't be one of those people!

Burnett, Richard E. *Karl Barth's Theological Exegesis.* Grand Rapids: Eerdmans, 2004.

This is hands down one of the most insightful books on Barth as a biblical exegete. The book is based on Burnett's doctoral thesis and examines how Barth did exegesis in the two editions of his *Romans* commentary. Burnett also gives insight into the various versions of the preface that Barth had prepared for the first edition of the commentary, which you won't find anywhere else. There's really nothing quite like Burnett's book in the English language, and readers will walk away not only richer in their knowledge of Barth but edified and challenged in their approach to doing scriptural exegesis in a truly theological manner.

McCormack, Bruce L. *Karl Barth's Critically Realistic Dialectical Theology: Its Genesis and Development, 1909–1936.* Oxford: Clarendon Press, 1995.

If you've paid attention to the notes in this book, you will likely have seen McCormack's book cited frequently. Indeed, it's difficult to work your way through an article or book published after 1995 that doesn't cite this truly seminal work. McCormack argues that Barth must be understood, from his break with liberalism in his earliest career until his death, consistently as a critically realistic dialectical theologian, despite different emphases or literary styles manifest in his work across the years. Impress your Barth professor by actually reading, digesting, and judiciously quoting McCormack's work!

Hunsinger, George. *How to Read Karl Barth: The Shape of His Theology.* New York; Oxford: Oxford University Press, 1991.

You may be surprised to see this book in the intermediate list, especially since the title implies that it would be aimed as an introduction. However, the book is really an attempt to provide a comprehensive interpretive framework for understanding Barth's theological project. Anyone interested in going on in Barth studies *must* read Hunsinger's book, especially because of how well he identifies six key motifs in Barth's thought. They are as follows: (1) *actualism*— Barth is more interested in understanding what God has actually done in history than what he is able to or might do; (2) *particularism*—Barth understands that it's more important to understand the particular outworkings of God's action (especially the incarnation) than making generalized or universalized statements about God; (3) *objectivism*—theological claims must be shaped by how God really is and reveals himself, not by the categories that fit better with our own era or perception of reality; (4) *personalism*— "God" is not simply a concept for a theological system but a living being who is really and personally encountered; (5) *realism*—theological language is capable of saying something real and significant about God, even if language itself cannot fully comprehend God; and (6) *rationalism*—Barth believes that language can say something coherent about God even while acknowledging that God continues to be mysterious and beyond full comprehension.[3]

Webster, John, ed. *The Cambridge Companion to Karl Barth.* Cambridge, UK: Cambridge University Press, 2000.

The best thing about this collection of essays on Karl Barth is that all eighteen provide both an overview but also in-depth insight on the

---

[3]For a short discussion of each of these motifs, see David Guretzki, "Become Conversant with Barth's Church Dogmatics: A Primer," in *Karl Barth in Conversation*, ed. W. Travis McMaken and David W. Congdon (Eugene, OR: Wipf & Stock, 2014), 286-87.

various facets of Barth's thought and theology. If you're planning to write a paper on some topic of Barth, there's a good chance that there's an essay in this collection that will either be worth quoting or will at least give you a good start in your study. Each essay also includes a short bibliography of works worth referencing for each topic.

Other Karl Barth Resources

Alexander Street Digital Karl Barth Library: *http://alexander street.com/products/digital-karl-barth-library*
The Alexander Street publisher has made most of Barth's *Gesamtausgabe* ("Collected Works") available in a digital format, as well as other works by Barth. It comprises forty-two volumes of Barth's writings, lectures, sermons, letters, and interviews, including the entire *Kirchliche Dogmatik (Church Dogmatics)* in German and English. Be sure to check your local university or seminary to see if they have a license to access these works.

Barth Literature Search Project: *http://barth.mediafiler.org /barth/index_Eng.htm*
The Barth Literature Search Project is a cooperative effort between *Zeitschrift für dialektische Theologie (Journal of Dialectical Theology)* at the Protestant Theological University in the Netherlands and the Center for Barth Studies at Princeton Theological Seminary. It provides an online database devoted explicitly to Karl Barth studies. The database covers literature in German, English, and Dutch.

Center for Barth Studies: *http://barth.ptsem.edu*
Princeton Theological Seminary houses the largest collection of Barth resources outside of the official Karl Barth Archive in Switzerland. Besides its extensive collection of primary and secondary sources on site, the Center has many online resources (book reviews, syllabi on Barth courses, media clips, etc.), sponsors an

annual Karl Barth conference, and supports symposia and workshops for graduate students and Barth translators.

Karl Barth-Archiv: *https://karlbarth.unibas.ch*
The official webpage of the Karl Barth Archive in Basel, Switzerland. Most of this page is in German, so it may not be of greatest use for non-German speakers. However, there is a treasure trove of materials available here.

Karl Barth Reading Room, Tyndale Seminary: *www.tyndale* *.ca/seminary/mtsmodular/reading-rooms/theology/barth*
A labor of love created and managed by Dr. Arnold Neufeld-Fast, a Tyndale Seminary (Toronto, Canada) professor and Barth scholar/ translator. The site includes handy links to primary and secondary Barth sources available online, multimedia and audio links, and an excellent list of published and unpublished dissertations, often with full-text links, on Karl Barth.

Logos Research Systems: *www.logos.com*
Logos is well-known for its Bible study software and its ongoing work of making classic texts of Christianity available in digital format. They have the full English text of the *CD* available along with a selection of many other of Barth's titles. They also offer a good selection of important secondary works as well. Go to the main page and simply search for "Karl Barth."

Index

About the Author

David Guretzki, PhD (McGill University) is Professor of Theology, Church, and Public life at Briercrest College and Seminary in Caronport, Saskatchewan, Canada. David has been teaching theology at Briercrest since 1993. He completed his PhD at McGill University in 2006 and wrote a thesis on Karl Barth, which was subsequently published by Ashgate as *Karl Barth on the Filioque* (2009). He is coauthor of IVP's *Pocket Dictionary of Theological Terms* and author of numerous chapters, articles, and reviews. Since 2006, he has facilitated a weekly Karl Barth reading group that meets throughout the academic year. He also enjoys attending the annual Karl Barth conference at Princeton Theological Seminary and has presented at the conference itself.

David has been involved in various aspects of theological engagement in public life. He has served as president of the Canadian Evangelical Theological Association, is a national board member of the Evangelical Fellowship of Canada, and has served as an "expert witness" in two legal cases in Canada dealing with matters of religious freedom.

David is married to Maureen, and together they have three children, Joey, Chiante, and Sierra. When David isn't teaching theology, he enjoys reading, astronomy, astrophotography, amateur radio, and occasional woodworking.

Finding the Textbook You Need

The IVP Academic Textbook Selector
is an online tool for instantly finding the IVP books
suitable for over 250 courses across 24 disciplines.

---

ivpacademic.com